GASTRIC BYPASS
COOKBOOK

Bariatric Recipes to Lose Weight after Bypass Surgery

HARPER EVANS

© **Copyright 2022 - All rights reserved.**

The content contained within this book may not be reproduced, duplicated, or transmitted without direct written permission from the author or the publisher.

Under no circumstances will any blame or legal responsibility be held against the publisher, or author, for any damages, reparation, or monetary loss due to the information contained within this book. Either directly or indirectly.

Legal Notice

This book is copyright protected. This book is only for personal use. You cannot amend, distribute, sell, use, quote, or paraphrase any part, or the content within this book, without the consent of the author or publisher.

Disclaimer Notice

Please note the information contained within this document is for educational and entertainment purposes only. All effort has been executed to present accurate, up-to-date, and reliable, complete information. No warranties of any kind are declared or implied. Readers acknowledge that the author is not engaging in the rendering of legal, financial, medical, or professional advice. The content within this book has been derived from various sources. Please consult a licensed professional before attempting any techniques outlined in this book.

By reading this document, the reader agrees that under no circumstances is the author responsible for any losses, direct or indirect, which are incurred as a result of the use of the information contained within this document, including, but not limited to, — errors, omissions, or inaccuracies.

Contents

Introduction 1

Chapter 1 Gastric Bypass Surgery 2

Chapter 2 What to Eat After a Gastric Bypass Surgery? 7

Chapter 3 Diet and Care After Bypass 15

Chapter 4 Stage 1 Diet: Clear Liquids 20

Chapter 5 Stage 2 Diet: Full Liquids/Pureed Foods 34

Chapter 6 Stage 3 Diet: Semi-Solid/Soft Foods 43

Chapter 7 Stage 4 Diet: Breakfast Recipes 56

Chapter 8 Meat and Seafood Recipes 83

Chapter 9 Vegetable Recipes 114

Chapter 10 Soups Recipes 130

Chapter 11 Snack and Appetizers Recipes 148

Chapter 12 Desserts Recipes 174

Conclusion 195

Introduction

For those who need to lose weight, gastric bypass surgery is a popular option. Others are required to have surgery because their doctor has told them to. You must adhere to a specific lifestyle and dietary regimen after the procedure, just like with any other sort of surgery. Let's first define the procedure to better comprehend the modifications you would need to make to your lifestyle.

When you undergo gastric bypass surgery, the size of your stomach shrinks, and you can no longer eat what you used to. During the surgery, the doctor will route your digestive tract or bypass it, so your body cannot absorb as much food as it used to. While gastric bypass surgery can help you lose weight, it also has some risks.

Gastric bypass surgery is a medical procedure that can help obese people lose weight and improve their health. It makes weight loss simpler by shrinking the stomach and changing how the stomach and small intestine absorb food. A Roux-en-Y gastric bypass is another name for this procedure.

Your safety. While your stomach is healing, certain meals may cause more stress. Establishing a new eating regimen that prioritizes protein. Fortunately, after surgery, your appetite levels change fast, and most individuals don't feel hungry in the same way they did before surgery, making it easier to manage your appetite.

Since it has been used for more than 30 years to treat severe obesity, gastric bypass is now thought to be the best option. The patient may lead a normal life, has no diarrhea, and just needs vitamin supplements. It is a safe technique with minimum morbidity and mortality, good long-term outcomes in terms of weight reduction and control of obesity-related illnesses, and fantastic quality of life.

This book will be there for you every step of the way, whether you are thinking about having surgery, are planning to have surgery, or have already had surgery.

Let's get started!

Chapter 1
Gastric Bypass Surgery

Gastric bypass is a type of weight-loss surgery that involves creating a small pouch from the stomach and linking this small pouch directly to the small intestine. It is also called "Roux-en-Y" gastric bypass. After the surgery, the foods swallowed will go into the small pouch created from the stomach and then directly into the small intestine, bypassing the major parts of the stomach and the first section of the small intestine. Gastric bypass is very common and is mostly done when diets and exercises haven't been effective in reducing weight for an individual. Another common instance where the gastric bypass is usually done is when an individual faces serious health issues as a result of being overweight.

As part of the treatment, food absorption is lowered and restricted. At the level of the lower curve of the stomach, a tiny reservoir with a capacity of around 30 to 35 ml is produced for this, dividing the remainder of the stomach (restrictive component). Food cannot flow through a large amount of the stomach, duodenum, and initial part of the small intestine since this reservoir is also connected to the small intestine (malabsorptive component).

Due to the poor capacity of the stomach, which fills up quickly, and the fact that digested foods do not travel through the digestive tract and do not come into contact with gastric, pancreatic, or bile juices in part of this route, the patient feels satisfied after eating less, and the amount of nutrients absorbed from digested foods is decreased (malabsorptive component). This process affects hormones as well. It lessens the production of ghrelin and gastric inhibitor peptides, which are associated with increased triglyceride synthesis in adipose tissue, increased insulin secretion, and increased hunger in morbidly obese individuals.

The quantity of weight loss varies and depends on the patient's behavior throughout the intervention, thus it is important to constantly monitor both food intake and physical activity. After surgery, there is a larger loss of weight in the first year, and after 5 years, there has been a 60–75% decline in weight.

The gastric bypass carries several complications, including the possibility of mortality in about 0.35% of patients. But, according to doctors, the patient's health advantages outweigh the danger because his chance of dying from a cardiovascular accident is lowered greatly with this treatment, and the weight reduction gained is significant. It enables the reduction and management of morbid obesity-related risk factors.

For this reason, these patients must provide sufficient assurances that they will continue post-surgery treatment, which entails a re-education work on their life habits (diet and physical exercise) that must be maintained for longer than one or two years required to lose excess weight. This is why, to receive this form of treatment, individuals had to complete a battery of medical examinations and psychological training because otherwise, the benefit-risk connection would be inverted.

Benefits of Gastric Bypass

- Higher life expectancy: People who are morbidly obese have a decreased life expectancy due to the increased risk of cardiovascular illness and death as well as other diseases, such as cancer, for which obesity is a risk factor.
- They regain the ability to perform routine chores, from the most elementary—like dressing—to the most complex—like fostering more and more fulfilling social interaction.
- A significant boost in your self-esteem as a result of your ability to lose weight and keep it off as well as your ability to lead a healthier and more fulfilling life.

Gastric Balloon, Gastric Band, Gastric Bypass

Weight loss can be for cosmetic or health reasons. When overweight is extreme, or there is an obesity problem, it is possible that eating a balanced diet and exercising will not be enough to lose all of the pounds that are threatening a person's health.

Surgical intervention may be the best option in certain situations. There are several types of obesity operations, but practically all are based on the same principle: limit the stomach's ability so that the sense of satiety occurs before eating less.

Other slimming procedures include cosmetic surgery, which involves changing the look but not the underlying problem, and is frequently performed on people who do not have a major health condition.

Intragastric Balloon

It involves inserting a balloon into the stomach and filling it with the serum to lower its capacity by around half, resulting in the same sense of satisfaction with less food, a caloric deficit, and calories collected in the form of body fat being consumed.

It is typically a simple procedure that may be conducted without anesthetic and the need for hospitalization. The balloon is placed through the nasogastric (a tube that enters the nose) and travels to the stomach, inflated and shut.

It stays there for roughly 6 months, and it's common to lose one kilo every week; however, this varies a lot from person to person. Ideally, spend that time on nutritional reeducation, taking advantage of even the tiniest hint of hunger to eat more healthily.

Gastric Band

Although easy, the gastric band procedure is a little more intrusive than the prior one. In this situation, an inflatable band is wrapped around the top region of the stomach, gently compressing it and creating two chambers where before there was just one as if we had two stomachs. Food falls into the first of these chambers when eating and eventually moves into the second through the gap created by the band. As a result, fullness sets in before long, and the stomach cannot grow to accommodate additional food from the bill.

Furthermore, the band can expand and deflate multiple times. It normally swells once inserted, and the necessity to swell it again and continue with food re-education is reevaluated after many weeks or months of treatment.

Gastric Sleeve

Because it needs general anesthesia, this procedure is more complex and riskier than the others. It involves stapling the stomach, which reduces its capacity by around 70%. The functional section is shaped like a banana and connects the esophagus to the gut.

Gastric Bypass

It's the most intrusive and, in most cases, the most successful method. It involves directly connecting the top section of the stomach to the small intestine, substantially limiting the area available for the food we consume, resulting in considerably quicker satiety and lower calorie intake.

A general anesthetic is required for hospitalization, and recovery takes longer.

Tummy Tuck or Liposuction

These procedures do not modify the digestive system; instead, they focus on removing body fat, which is why they are purely cosmetic.

A stomach tuck involves lifting the skin of the abdomen and removing the accumulated fat beneath it, and reinforcing the muscles if they are excessively flaccid. It's a fairly intrusive procedure requiring general anesthesia and a lengthy recovery period that can be uncomfortable.

A local anesthetic is used to inject a syringe that absorbs excess fat from any portion of the body that you wish to remove in a liposuction procedure. Recovery time is reduced, and hospitalization is rarely required.

Because there is no interference on the digestive system in either situation, it is a pointless procedure if habits are not modified, as the fat removed may be replaced.

For Whom Is It Suitable?

Anyone who is overweight should not contemplate undergoing a weight-loss procedure. The first steps should always be focused on changing one's lifestyle and, in certain cases, treating medical disorders that may be causing weight gain, such as hypothyroidism.

Obese persons are the most likely candidates for these therapies, especially with type 2 diabetes. They must be informed of the dangers and advantages of the intervention and the fact that, in addition to the intervention, they must commit to a lifestyle change, particularly in their eating habits.

These sorts of surgeries are not commonly performed on children and teenagers. When they are considered, they have morbid obesity at a young age, with a BMI of at least 35, which can jeopardize their health more than the procedure itself.

It's important to remember that any surgical procedure contains some risk, no matter how little, especially when the local anesthetic is used. Undergoing one must be a well-thought-out, medically justified decision, and the patient must be aware of the dangers involved.

In the event of the procedures above, except purely aesthetic surgeries, stomach discomfort, nausea, or vomiting, ulcers, wound infection, and bleeding may occur, in addition to the inherent hazards of any surgery.

In many situations, however, morbid obesity or excessive overweight poses a higher health danger than any surgery: heart and circulation difficulties, respiratory problems, joint impact, trouble moving, and leading a normal life are only a few of the consequences of a major weight gain.

Aesthetic procedures aside (which can be completely ineffective if no behavioral changes are made), weight reduction surgeries are not a magic solution for weight loss without effort. All are centered on reducing the stomach size so that the patient may eat less without becoming hungry, but they will not assist in the long run unless the patient undergoes a dietary re- education.

Because the stomach might enlarge after surgery, it is critical to use the months after the procedure to establish new food habits and begin exercising. Consequently, despite the danger, the trip to the operating room will provide long-term benefits and will have been beneficial.

Chapter 2
What to Eat After a Gastric Bypass Surgery?

Do you have any concerns about your post-surgery diet? Learn about the foods that can help you heal and healthily lose weight. People suffering from sleeve gastrostomy and gastric bypass surgery, also known as Roux Y gastric bypass, can use a gastric bypass diet to rehabilitate and adjust their eating habits. Your doctor or a certified dietitian will go through the post-surgery diet with you, including what foods you can eat and how much you may eat at each meal. If you keep to your gastric bypass diet, you may lose weight safely.

The goal of the gastric bypass diet is to:

- Allow your stomach to recover without having to stretch your meals
- Get in the habit of consuming the tiniest quantities of food that your tiniest stomach can easily and securely digest
- Assist you in reducing weight and avoiding weight gain
- Minimize the negative effects and consequences of surgery

Liquids

You will only be able to drink clear liquids for the first 24 hours after surgery. You can start drinking different liquids once you've become used to clear liquids, such as:

- Broth
- Sugar-free juice
- Tea or coffee that has been decaffeinated
- Jelly or sugar-free ice cream popsicles
- Milk (skim or 1%fat)

Pureed Foods

You can start eating strained and pureed meals after approximately a week of tolerating liquids. Without substantial particles of food in the combination, the meal must have the consistency of a soft paste or a thick liquid.

It is sufficient to eat 3 to 6 small meals every day. At each meal, 4 to 6 tsp of food should be ingested. Slow down and enjoy your food: each meal should last about 30 minutes. Select items that purée well, such as:

- Lean ground beef, chicken, or fish
- Curd
- Scrambled eggs that aren't too firm
- Cereal that has been cooked
- Cooked veggies and soft fruits
- Soups made with poured cream

Mix solid foods with a liquid, such as:

- Water
- Skim milk
- Juice without added sugar
- Broth

Soft Foods

After a few weeks of ingesting pureed foods and with your doctor's approval, you can add soft foods to your diet. Small, delicate, and easy-to-chew chunks are ideal. 3 to 5 modest pieces each day are plenty. A ⅓ cup of food should be consumed at each meal. Before swallowing, chew each bite until the food is pureed.

- Lean ground beef or chicken are examples of soft meals
- Fish that has been shredded
- Eggs
- Curd

- Cereal, cooked or dry
- Rice
- Cooked veggies, skinless
- Fresh soft, or canned fruits, without seeds or skin

Solid Foods

You can gradually return to eating harder foods after around 8 weeks on the gastric post-bypass diet. Begin by eating 3 meals every day. 1 to 1 ½ cups of food should be served to each person. It's critical to quit eating before you're entirely satisfied.

You may change the number of meals and the amount of food in each meal depending on how well you handle solid foods. Consult your dietician to determine what is best for you.

One by one, try new foods. Some meals might induce discomfort, nausea, and vomiting following gastric bypass surgery.

The following foods can pose issues at this stage:

- Bread
- Soft drinks
- Raw vegetables
- Hard meats or meats with cartilage
- Red meat
- Fried food
- Cooked fibrous vegetables
- Spicy or spicy foods
- Nuts and seeds
- Popcorn

With the help of your doctor, you may be able to try some of these foods again in the future.

A New Healthy Diet

The size of your stomach is reduced, and the manner food enters your intestines is altered during gastric bypass surgery. After surgery, you must eat properly while keeping up with your weight loss goals. The doctor is likely to recommend that:

- Eat and drink slowly. Allow 30 minutes to eat and 30 to 60 minutes to drink 1 cup of liquid to avoid fast gastric evacuation syndrome. Drinking liquids should be done 30 minutes before or after each meal.
- Eat small amounts. Throughout the day, eat many small meals. You can begin with eating 6 little meals per day, then 4, and eventually 3 meals per day if you keep a normal diet. 1 cup of food should be served at each meal.
- Drink fluids between meals. To avoid dehydration, drink at least 8 cups (1.9 liters) of fluids daily. However, drinking too many fluids during or close to meals might make you feel bloated and prevent consuming enough nutrient-dense foods.
- Chew food completely. The new opening that goes from the stomach to the small intestine is very narrow and blocked with large pieces of food. Food cannot leave the stomach, resulting in vomiting, nausea, and abdominal pain. Before swallowing, take small bites of food and chew them until they are consistent.
- Prioritize protein foods. Eat these foods before eating other foods in your meal.
- Foods heavy in fat and sugar should be avoided. These meals quickly pass through your digestive tract, resulting in rapid gastric evacuation syndrome.
- Take the recommended vitamin and mineral supplements. After surgery, your body will not absorb enough nutrients from food. You may need to take a multivitamin supplement every day for the rest of your life.

The gastric bypass diet might help you get back on your feet after surgery, gradually adopt healthy eating, and achieve weight loss goals. Remember that if you resume unhealthy eating habits after weight loss surgery, you may not lose all excess weight or recover the weight you have lost.

What Are the Possible Side Effects of a Gastric Bypass?

Like any surgery, a gastric bypass carries risks. We will also inform you extensively about this during the preliminary phase. The following side effects can occur with a gastric bypass.

Seam Leakage

During the operation, the surgeon makes new connections. For example, the connection between the new stomach and the small intestine. Those connections can leak. This is most common around the stomach. Sometimes this is because a patient eats more than what fits in the new small stomach. We can easily solve a seam leak. Reoperation or gastroscopy is then required. All patients who have had an anastomotic leak have recovered well.

Throwing up

Shortly after the operation, the stomach may swell slightly. This can narrow the passage from your new small stomach to the small intestine. It is possible that this will cause you to vomit. The swelling will disappear on its own in the days after surgery. This will make you throw up a lot less or not at all.

Do the complaints persist? Then we usually make an X-ray of the stomach. Sometimes it is necessary to perform a gastroscopy. During this examination, the Gastroenterologist and Liver Doctor searches for the narrowing with a

camera. If possible, he widens the constriction. Food can then move more easily from the stomach to the small intestine.

Gallstones

You will lose weight quickly after surgery. This puts you at a higher risk of gallstones.

Dumping

Dumping occurs when products with a lot of calories (with a lot of sugars, fats or carbohydrates) reach the small intestine too quickly. Your blood then goes to the intestines, which lowers blood pressure in the brain. This makes you sleepy or dizzy. Hormones associated with this can cause palpitations. This can make you sweat and lower your blood pressure. When this happens, stay calm, lie down and drink a glass of water if necessary. It will go away on its own after about 1 hour. Try to discover how the dumping could have come about. If you experience this problem more often, please contact one of our employees. Having a dump is definitely annoying. But you can also see it as a tool. It prevents you from taking (too many) high-calorie products again in the future.

Vitamin Deficiency

Due to the diversion of (a large part of your) digestive tract, you can no longer absorb certain vitamins properly. The quantities per meal are also small. As a result, you may not get enough of some vitamins. We therefore always recommend taking vitamins for life. These are specially made for patients who have a gastric bypass.

Internal Herniation

After a gastric bypass, there is a small risk of getting an internal herniation. Openings are created in the inner abdominal wall. The small intestine can become trapped in such an opening. This is then an internal herniation. You have abdominal pain that comes and goes; sometimes you have it every day, but sometimes it is also absent for several days or weeks. Surgery is needed to clear the entrapment and close the openings. Nowadays, the openings are already closed during the gastric bypass operation. This reduces the risk of internal herniation. It is now about 2 to 5%. Risks and solutions of the stomach bypass

As with any major operation, gastric bypass and other weight-loss procedures have a risk of health complications, both short and long-term.

Others:

- Excessive bleeding
- Infection

- Long-term risks and complications associated with gastric bypass surgery include the following:
- Bowel obstruction
- Gallstones
- Hernias
- Low blood sugar (hypoglycemia)
- Malnutrition
- Stomach perforation
- Ulcers
- Occasionally, gastric bypass complications can be fatal

Your post-op nutritional plan will be different from the one you had before deciding to have gastric bypass surgery.

Dietary Recommendations

You might be shocked to find that even after a tiny lunch, you feel full. This is a result of your stomach getting smaller and your small intestine or bowel getting shorter. Your surgeon will advise you to limit the amount and type of food you eat for the first few days after the procedure since your internal wounds need time to heal.

You must develop the practice of eating thoroughly and slowly. Do not be shocked if you vomit or feel nauseated if you are eager to consume everything on your plate as quickly as possible.

Guidelines for Liquids

Similar to the consumption of solid foods, even liquids must be drunk very slowly. Do remember that they have to undergo digestion too.

Never combine water or drinks with meals. Concerning water, please consume it 30 minutes or an hour before a meal. Alternatively, you may wait for an hour or so after your meal before drinking water. Otherwise, you are bound to experience nausea and vomiting. Your stomach may expand and even rupture.

This does not mean that you have to avoid liquids or keep them to a minimum. Please consume loads of fluids. It would be best if you had them to keep your body well-hydrated. You can even become dehydrated through frequent bouts of diarrhea or vomiting. Therefore, ensure that you consume at least 3 to 4 ounces of water between meals. You may even go in for acceptable low-calorie beverages.

Other Guidelines

3 days of hospitalization should suffice after your Gastric Bypass operation. You may develop life-threatening blood clots. To prevent this, your surgeon will advise you not to keep lying down in bed but to sit in a chair for as long as possible. Additionally, even if you are in pain, you will be forced to walk around, albeit with assistance. This is to ensure healthy blood circulation.

Since the newly created connections in your digestive system need time to heal, you will not be permitted to eat or drink anything on the day of the surgery. The next day, you may be allowed to take sips of water. After that, you will be advised on the various phases of a pre-determined dietary regimen that you must follow for healthy recovery and weight loss maintenance.

If your condition is good, you will be discharged after 3 days. Please adhere to the follow-up schedule charted out for you. The first follow-up will be a couple of weeks after your surgery. If you experience frequent vomiting, nausea, fever, chills, or worsening pain in the first two weeks, please request an emergency consultation with your Bariatric surgeon. Do the same if your incisions show signs of painful inflammation.

Chapter 3
Diet and Care After Bypass

Supplemental Calcium

It is possible to avoid calcium deficiency and bone disease by consuming 1,200 to 2,000 milligrams of calcium each day. To improve absorption, consume calcium in two to 3 divided doses throughout the day, such as a 500 to 600 mg supplement 3 times per day. The calcium type that is advised is calcium citrate.

Dietary Changes Following Bariatric Surgery

For the first few days after surgery, you will only be able to consume clear liquids. After leaving the hospital, it is possible to gradually add thicker beverages to your diet.

Foods that have been blended or puréed may be introduced two weeks after surgery. During this time, you can satisfy your protein needs by consuming liquid supplements that are high in protein (more than 20 g) and low in calories (less than 200 calories).

It's important to keep in mind that, after surgery, your stomach is quite small —less than ¼ cup, or about the size of an egg. The opening through which food leaves your stomach is also quite small. It is crucial to consume no more than two to 3 bites or sips of any new meal at once and to wait 10 minutes before doing so. This will help you decide what your tolerance and boundary levels are. Your stomach will empty more quickly from liquids than from soft solids.

If you overeat or eat too quickly, you might experience pain or nausea. Steer clear of creamy, rich liquids like ice cream, gravies, and sauces.

Fluids

- To prevent dehydration in between meals, drink more water and calorie- free or low-calorie liquids. In all liquids, caffeine should be avoided.
- Drink about 1 cup of liquid between each small meal.

- We advise a minimum daily hydration intake of 2 liters (64 ounces or 8 cups). You'll be able to accomplish this objective eventually.
- We strongly discourage consuming alcoholic beverages. Following surgery, alcohol enters your system much more quickly, making its sedative and mood-altering effects harder to predict and manage.

Multivitamins

Selenium, copper, zinc, selenium, 400 mcg of folic acid and at least 18 mg of iron are all required in a daily chewable multivitamin and mineral supplement. This formula is used in both Centrum Adult chewable multivitamins and Trader Joe's. After surgery, take two pills each day for at least 3 months before switching to one pill per day for the rest of your life.

Supplements

You must regularly take the following supplements to prevent vitamin deficiencies. Please keep in mind that every tablet needs to be broken up into 6 to 8 little pieces. Because of your altered anatomy, you may not be able to absorb complete tablets as well as you could have before surgery.

General Guidelines

- Consume well-balanced meals in small portions.
- Consume a low-calorie, low-fat, and sugar-sweetened diet.
- Keep track of your daily meal portions and calorie and protein intake.
- Consume slowly and thoroughly chew little bits of food.
- Rice, bread, raw vegetables, and fresh fruits, as well as tough-to-chew meats like pig and steak, should be avoided. Ground meats are generally more tolerable.
- Avoid straws, carbonated beverages, and ice-chewing. They have the potential to introduce air into your pouch, causing pain.

- Avoid sugar, foods, and beverages containing sugar, concentrated sweets, and fruit juices.
- During the first two months following surgery, you should consume between 300 and 600 calories per day, emphasizing thin and thick liquids, according to the American College of Nutrition.
- A daily caloric intake of no more than 1,000 calories is recommended.

After surgery, you will receive clear liquids such as juices, Jell-O, and broth as your first meal. Although fluid and Jell-O contain a lot of sugar, your servings will be pretty minimal at this point. Increase the amount of liquid you drink at each meal gradually as tolerated.

Diet for the First Two Weeks Post-Surgery

You'll begin by incorporating thicker beverages high in protein but low in fat and sugar. You can drink high-protein, low-calorie supplement drinks or powders to meet your protein needs during this time.

The objective is to consume little servings that conveniently fit into your pouch. Begin with portion sizes of 1 tbsp and gradually increase to 2 tbsp as tolerated. Start with ¼ cup of liquid and gradually increase to ½ cup as tolerated. Caloric intake should not exceed 400 calories per day.

Additionally, it is critical to maintaining proper hydration. Daily, drink between 1 and 1.5 liters of water or other non-caloric liquids.

Recommended thicker liquids:

- Nonfat or 1% milk, if you can handle milk
- Low-calorie lactose-free or soy-based beverages
- Pudding without sugar
- Yogurt that is sugar-free and fat-free
- Cottage cheese with a low-fat content
- Soup made with blended broth or other low-fat soups

Hot cereals have been refined and are deficient in fiber, such as creams of rice or wheat. Add additional liquid to achieve a soup-like consistency. Consume no oatmeal.

Optional liquid supplements with high protein content and a low-calorie count (An 8- to 11-ounce serving has fewer than 200 calories and more than 20 g of protein).

To increase your protein intake, mix 2 tsp of nonfat dry milk powder, egg substitute, powdered egg, or other protein powder into each ½ cup of nonfat or low-fat milk. Additionally, you can add them to thick liquids like soups and hot cereal.

Drink 1 cup of water or other non-caloric drinks in between meals. Take a multivitamin supplement each day. Diet for Weeks 2 to 4 Post-Surgery.

As tolerated, begin adding tiny amounts of puréed and soft meals. Take tiny chunks and chew thoroughly. When introducing a new dish, take no more than two nibbles every 20 minutes.

Suggestions for puréed and soft foods:

- Applesauce
- Yogurt
- Cheesy cottage
- Vegetables that have been thoroughly cooked and puréed
- Cereals chaudes
- Potatoes mashed
- Noodles
- Egg whites scrambled or egg
- Replacement
- Fruits in cans
- Tuna in cans
- Lean fish
- Ground meats or poultry that is lean

- Avoid all bread and hard-to-chew meats

Weekly Meal Plan Recommendation for Weeks 2 to 8 Until 2 Months Post-Surgery

At this point, your daily caloric intake should not exceed 500 calories, distributed between 6 to 8 quick meals. The suggested portion size for solids is ¼ cup and for liquids is ½ cup.

Long-Term Dietary Guidelines

With time, you'll be able to add more variety and consistency to your diet. Certain meals, such as red meat, chicken, bread, and high-fiber fruits and vegetables, may continue to be poorly tolerated. Maintain a low-fat, low- sugar, and low-calorie diet and continue to track your daily calorie intake. If you are using the 900 to 1,000-calorie diet plan stated above, try to reach your serving goals for all food groups.

To maintain proper hydration, consume at least 2 liters of water or non- caloric fluids daily unless a medical condition precludes this.

Chapter 4
Stage 1 Diet: Clear Liquids

Tips

A clear liquid diet comprises clear liquids such as water, broth, and plain gelatin that are readily digested and leave no unprocessed residue in the intestine. Before certain medical operations or if you have specific

digestive difficulties, your doctor may prescribe a clear liquid diet. Due to the inability of a transparent liquid diet to supply appropriate calories and nutrients, it should not be used for more than a few days.

Clear drinks and meals may be colored as long as they remain transparent. Liquid foods are those that partially or melt into liquid at normal temperature. While on a clear liquid diet, you cannot consume solid food.

Purpose

A clear liquid diet is frequently utilized prior to examinations, operations, or surgeries that do not require the presence of food in the stomach or intestines, such as colonoscopy. Additionally, it may be recommended as a short-term diet if you are experiencing certain digestive disorders, such as nausea, vomiting, or diarrhea, or if you are recovering from certain types of surgery.

A clear liquid diet assists in maintaining enough hydration supplies essential electrolytes such as salt and potassium and offers energy when a complete food is not possible or suggested.

In general, the following items are permitted on a clear liquid diet:

- Aqua (plain, carbonated, or flavored)
- Juices from fruits that do not contain pulp, such as apple or white grape juice
- Beverages with a fruit flavor, such as fruit punch or lemonade
- Carbonated drinks, such as dark sodas (cola and root beer)

Banana Cream Protein Shake

Preparation Time: 10 minutes

Cooking Time: 0 minutes

Servings: 2

Ingredients

- 1 ½ cups low-fat milk
- ¼ cup low-fat, plain Greek yogurt
- 1 small banana
- 1 tsp vanilla extract
- 1 scoop (¼ cup) vanilla protein powder
- 1 tbsp sugar-free instant banana pudding mix

Directions

1. Combine the milk, yogurt, banana, vanilla, protein powder, and pudding mix in a blender.
2. Blend on high for 2 to 3 minutes, until the powder has dissolved and the mixture is smooth. Serve and enjoy!

Nutrition: Calories: 226, Fat: 4 g, Protein: 17 g, Carbs: 30 g, Cholesterol: 23 mg

Chocolate Cherry Smoothie

Preparation Time: 10 minutes
Cooking Time: 0 minutes
Servings: 2
Ingredients

- 1 cups frozen cherries
- 1 cup unsweetened almond milk
- 2 tbsp raw cacao powder
- 1 scoop protein powder, plain, (optional)

Directions

1. Add full ingredients to a blender and blend until smooth, adding more milk if necessary.
2. Serve and enjoy.

Nutrition: Calories: 190, Carbs: 20 g, Fat: 11 g, Protein: 6 g, Cholesterol: 12 mg

Fat-Free Chicken Broth

Preparation Time: 10 minutes

Cooking Time: 40 minutes

Servings: 1

Ingredients

- Black pepper, to taste
- Salt, to taste
- 1 whole chicken
- Garlic powder, to taste

Directions

1. Add all ingredients with enough water to completely cover the chicken in a pot.
2. Let it boil; keep skimming the bubbles on top. Keep in the fridge for 2 hours, and skim the fat off. Serve and save the rest for another use.

Nutrition: Calories: 327, Protein: 45 g, Carbs: 6 g, Fat: 105 g, Cholesterol: 11 mg

High Protein Milk

Preparation Time: 5 minutes
Cooking Time: 0 minutes
Servings: 1
Ingredients

- ¼ tsp vanilla extract
- ½ cup (4 oz.) Low-fat milk
- 2 scoops unflavored protein powder

Directions

1. Combine all fixings in your blender and process until smooth.
2. Serve and enjoy.

Nutrition: Calories: 140, Protein: 24 g, Carbs: 6g, Fat: 1 g, Cholesterol: 12 mg

Lemon Pie Protein Shake

Preparation Time: 5 minutes

Cooking Time: 10 minutes

Servings: 1

Ingredients

- 1 cup low-fat milk
- 1 package sugar-free hot chocolate mix
- 1 scoop (¼ cup) unflavored protein powder

Directions

1. In your small saucepan over medium-low heat, whisk the milk, hot chocolate mix, and protein powder.
2. Whisk continuously just until warm, but do not boil. Pour into a heat-proof mug, and enjoy.

Nutrition: Calories: 254, Fat: 5 g, Protein: 28 g, Carbs: 23 g, Cholesterol: 11 mg

Chocolate-Mint Protein Shake

Preparation Time: 5 minutes
Cooking Time: 0 minutes
Servings: 2
Ingredients
- 1 cup low-fat milk
- ½ cup low-fat cottage cheese
- 1 scoop (¼ cup) chocolate protein powder
- 1 tbsp cocoa powder
- ¼ tsp mint extract
- 4 ice cubes

Directions
1. Combine the milk, cottage cheese, protein powder, cocoa powder, mint extract, and ice in your blender.
2. Blend on high until smooth. Serve and enjoy!

Nutrition: Calories: 170, Fat: 3 g, Protein: 19 g, Carbs: 15 g

Low-Fat Vegetable Broth

Preparation Time: 10 minutes
Cooking Time: 20 minutes
Servings: 1
Ingredients

- 3 oz chopped carrots
- 6 cups water
- 5 oz chopped green beans
- ½ tsp dried basil, thyme & sage
- 4 oz chopped celery
- 4 cubes low-sodium chicken stock

Directions

1. In a pot, add water and cubes, and let it come to a boil. Add the rest of the ingredients.
2. Let it boil again and simmer for 15 minutes. Strain and cool slightly, and serve.

Nutrition: Calories: 217, Protein: 34 g, Carbs: 5.3 g, Fat: 67.2 g, Cholesterol: 5 mg

Mango Pevery Smoothie

Preparation Time: 5 minutes
Cooking Time: 0 minutes
Servings: 2
Ingredients

- 1 ½ cups almond milk
- 1 cup chopped mango, fresh or frozen
- ½ tsp vanilla extract
- 1 cup ice

Directions

1. Blend almond milk, diced every, mango, and vanilla in a food processor or blender until smooth. Make a thorough mix.
2. Blend in the ice until it dissolves completely. If the mixture is too thin, add additional almond milk.

Nutrition: Calories: 120, Carbs: 22 g, Fat 2g, Protein: 4 g, Cholesterol: 0 mg

Piña Colada Protein Shake

Preparation Time: 5 minutes

Cooking Time: 0 minutes

Servings: 2

Ingredients

- 1 ½ cups unsweetened coconut milk
- ½ cup low-fat cottage cheese
- 1 cup frozen pineapple chunks
- 1 tsp coconut extract
- 1 scoop (¼ cup) vanilla protein powder
- 4 or 5 ice cubes
- Any sugar substitute, for added sweetness (optional)

Directions

1. In a blender, combine the coconut milk, cottage cheese, pineapple, coconut extract, protein powder, ice, and sugar substitute (if using).
2. Blend on high until smooth. Serve and enjoy!

Nutrition: Calories: 195, Fat: 5 g, Protein: 14 g, Carbs: 18 g, Cholesterol: 0 mg, Protein

Chai Latte With Coconut Milk Froth

Preparation Time: 5 minutes

Cooking Time: 0 minutes

Servings: 1

Ingredients

- 10 to 12 oz brewed chai tea
- 1 scoop cinnamon swirl whey Protein
- 2 tbsp light coconut milk
- 45 mg pure Stevia

Directions

1. Blend the chai tea with the whey protein in a blender bottle until smooth and mixed.
2. Pour the remaining chai mix into a mug and set aside 2 tbsp for serving.
3. Shake the reserved chai mixture well before adding the coconut milk and stevia. Serve and enjoy!

Nutrition: Calories: 155, Carbs: 8g, Fat 0g, Protein: 30g, Cholesterol: 12 mg

Sugar-Free Jell-O

Preparation Time: 10 minutes
Cooking Time: 20 minutes
Servings: 1
Ingredients

- ¼ cup strawberries
- ½ tbsp gelatin powder
- 2 cups water
- 3 tbsp no-calorie sweetener

Directions

1. In a pan, add strawberries and mix with water (half), and let it come to a boil. Keep mashing them. Simmer on low heat for 8 to 10 minutes.
2. In your bowl, add the rest of the water and mix with gelatin and let it rest for 5 minutes.
3. Pass the mashed strawberries throw a fine-mesh sieve, straining well. Add enough water to make it 3 cups.
4. In a pan, add strawberry juice and mix with a sugar substitute. Cook on low for 2 minutes, add gelatin and cook until it dissolves.
5. Pour into a baking dish and keep in the fridge for 5 to 6 hours. Slice and serve.

Nutrition: Calories: 232, Protein: 8 g, Carbs: 1.3 g, Fat: 1.4 g, Cholesterol: 12 mg

Vanilla Bean Protein Shake

Preparation Time: 10 minutes
Cooking Time: 0 minutes
Servings: 2
Ingredients
- 1 cup low-fat milk
- ½ cup low-fat, vanilla Greek yogurt
- 1 tsp vanilla extract
- 1 scoop (¼ cup) vanilla protein powder
- 4 ice cubes

Directions
1. Combine the milk, yogurt, vanilla, protein powder, and ice in a blender.
2. Blend on high for 2 to 3 minutes, until the protein powder has dissolved and the mixture is smooth.
3. Pour half of the shake into your glass, and enjoy.

Nutrition: Calories: 153, Fat: 2 g, Protein: 16 g, Carbs: 14 g, Cholesterol: 11 mg

Cocoa Almond Protein Smoothie

Preparation Time: 5 minutes
Cooking Time: 0 minutes
Servings: 1
Ingredients

- ¾ cup Greek yogurt
- ¼ cup + 2 tbsp milk
- 1 medium banana, sliced and frozen
- ½ tbsp unsweetened cocoa powder
- 2 tbsp almond butter
- 2 tsp ground flaxseed (optional)
- ¾ cup ice cubes

Directions

1. Blend full ingredients until smooth in the blender.
2. Serve and enjoy!

Nutrition: Calories: 120, Carbs: 15 g, Fat:6g, Protein: 5g, Cholesterol: 12 mg

Chapter 5
Stage 2 Diet: Full Liquids/Pureed Foods

Vanilla Chai Protein Shake

Preparation Time: 5 minutes
Cooking Time: 0 minutes
Servings: 2
Ingredients

- 1 scoop vanilla protein powder
- ½ cup chai tea
- ½ tsp ground nutmeg
- ½ tsp ground cardamom
- ½ cup unsweetened almond milk
- 1 cup ice

Directions

1. In a blender, combine all elements and blend on high for 1 to 2 minutes, or until desired consistency is achieved.
2. If your smoothie is overly thick, thin it up with additional milk or water.

Nutrition: Calories: 200, Fat: 12 g, Protein: 21 g, Carbs: 2 g, Cholesterol: 67 mg

Pineapple Coconut Smoothie

Preparation Time: 5 minutes

Cooking Time: 0 minutes

Servings: 2

Ingredients

- 3 cups frozen pineapple chunks, with a little extra for decoration
- ½ cup unsweetened coconut milk
- ½ cup pineapple juice
- 2 tbsp shredded, unsweetened coconut
- ½ cup yogurt vanilla
- 1 tbsp honey

Directions

1. Accumulate the components.
2. Combine all of the ingredients in a blender. Process until completely smooth.
3. Pineapple pieces can be used as garnish. Serve right away.

Tips: If you're trying to trim back on sugar, use unsweetened coconut milk, unsweetened shredded coconut, and unsweetened frozen pineapple chunks in this recipe. They are available at select health food and natural food retailers, including Whole Foods Market and Trader Joe's.

Recipe Variations: Substitute ½ cup plain yogurt for the vanilla yogurt and around ¼ tsp vanilla extract. For a lovely appearance, garnish each glass with a sprig of fresh mint.

Consider using agave syrup or a sugar alternative in place of honey. Use unsweetened coconut powder in place of flaked coconut.

How to store and freeze: If you have any leftover smoothies, cover them and store them in the refrigerator for up to 3 days.

Smoothies may also be frozen. Place the combination in an airtight container or a freezer bag with a zip-lock closure and freeze for up to 3 months.

Nutrition: Calories: 218, Protein: 21 g, Fat: 13 g, Carbs: 2 g, Cholesterol: 6 mg

Chocolate Protein Shake

Preparation Time: 5 minutes

Cooking Time: 0 minutes

Servings: 2

Ingredients

- ¾ cup unsweetened vanilla almond milk
- 1 scoop (¼ cup + 1 tbsp (32 g)) chocolate protein powder use a good- quality brand
- 1 tbsp Dutch-process cocoa powder (Hershey's Special Dark works well)
- ½ cup frozen banana (Note 1)
- 1 tbsp almond butter or peanut butter
- ¼ tsp vanilla extract, optional
- 8 ice cubes
- Optional: sweetener to taste (Note 2)

Directions

1. In advance: Remove the banana's skin, slice it into large coins, and freeze it in a plastic bag.
2. BLEND: In a high-powered blender, combine all of the ingredients. Blend until the mixture is smooth and all of the components are integrated. If necessary, whisk everything together and re-blend. If you don't have a powerful blender, an additional ¼ cup of milk may be required.
3. ENJOY: Pour into a glass and enjoy!

Recipe Notes

Note 1: Bananas: When bananas are completely ripe, coin them and place them in a small Ziplock bag. Freeze for at least 24 hours or until totally solid.

Note 2: Protein powder: Depending on the protein powder you use (some are sweetened with stevia), your shake may require additional sugar. I frequently add a few drops of stevia, maple syrup, or honey. Supplement with own preference.

Nutrition: Calories: 293, Carbs: 30 g, Protein: 22 g, Fat: 14 g, Sugar: 11 g, Cholesterol: 5 mg

Simple Egg Custard

Preparation Time: 5 minutes

Cooking Time: 0 minutes

Servings: 2

Ingredients

- 2 cups milk
- 1 tsp vanilla extract
- 4 egg yolks
- 1 tbsp cornflour
- 1 ½ tbsp sugar (optional)

Directions

1. In a little saucepan over medium heat, warm the milk and vanilla essence until just below the boiling point.
2. In a large separate basin, whisk together the egg yolks, cornflour, and sugar.
3. Whisk continually as you slowly pour the milk mixture into the egg yolks.
4. Return the milk and egg mixture to the saucepan and cook, stirring constantly to prevent the custard from sticking to the bottom, until the custard has thickened and coats the back of a spoon.
5. Serve instantly or chill for up to 2 days in the refrigerator.

Nutrition: Calories: 353, Fat: 21 g, Carbs: 20.5 g, Sugar: 8 g, Protein:25 g, Cholesterol: 54 mg

Watermelon and Strawberry Chia Smoothie

Preparation Time: 5 minutes
Cooking Time: 5 minutes
Servings: 2
Ingredients

- 2 cups watermelon
- 1 ½ cups low-fat vanilla yogurt
- ½ cup vanilla almond milk
- 3 tbsp Premier Protein Vanilla Whey Powder
- 2 tsp chia seeds
- 1 banana frozen
- 1 cup strawberries frozen

Directions

1. Blend all ingredients in a high-speed blender.
2. Begin at low speed and gradually raise to high speed for approximately 30 to 45 seconds, or until the mixture is creamy and lump-free.
3. If the combination is still too thick for your liking, gradually adding more milk can resolve the issue.
4. Divide between 2 tall glasses and, if wanted, sprinkle with additional chia seeds. Serve immediately.

Nutrition: Calories: 305, Carbs: 57 g, Protein: 12 g, Fat: 4 g, Sugar: 45 g, Cholesterol: 45 mg

Creamy Healthy Soup

Preparation Time: 5 minutes
Cooking Time: 30 minutes
Servings: 2
Ingredients

Healthy Creamy Soup Broth:

- 4 large zucchinis (700 g/1.2 lb) peeled and cut into 1.5cm/3/5" slices.
- ½ onion, finely chopped (brown, white, yellow)
- 2 garlic cloves, peeled and whole
- 2 cups coffee (500 ml) broth made from chicken (or veg broth)
- 2 cups (500 ml) filtered water
- Garlic powder and onion powder (each ½ tsp)
- ¼ tsp freshly ground black pepper
- 1 cup oats (250 ml) 0 % fat milk is available

Soup Add-Ins:

- 1 tbsp (15 g) butter or extra virgin olive oil
- 2 minced garlic cloves
- 1 large onion, peeled and finely chopped
- 1.5 cup peeled and coarsely diced carrot
- 1.5 cup finely chopped celery
- 1 small red bell pepper/capsicum, finely chopped
- 1.5 cup chopped cooked chicken breast
- ¾ cup peas, frozen

Garnish:

- Fresh thyme (high recommended, or sub chives)

Directions

1. Healthy Creamy Broth: In a saucepan, combine all Broth ingredients EXCEPT milk, cover with a lid, and bring to a vigorous simmer over medium-high heat.
2. Decrease to low heat and simmer for 15 minutes, or until the zucchinis are very tender.
3. Take the pan off the heat and add the milk. Blitz with a handheld blender until smooth. Season with salt to taste. Take note of the creamy broth's low- calorie count!

Healthy Cream of Chicken Soup:

4. Melt butter in a small saucepan or a large pot over medium heat.
5. Combine the garlic, onion, carrot, and celery in a medium bowl. Cook for
6. 3 minutes before adding the capsicum. Continue cooking for a further 2 minutes, or until the onion is transparent and delicious.
7. Combine the broth, chicken, and peas. Get to a medium simmer and cook for only 2–3 minutes, or until peas are tender.
8. Season with salt and pepper to taste.
9. Divide among bowls and garnish with a pinch of fresh thyme leaves. Devour, and wonder at how low in calories such a creamy, totally delectable cup of soup is!!

Recipe Notes:

Storage-broth will readily keep for 4 to 5 days in the refrigerator. While it may appear split, once heated, vigorously swirl and it will come together. Additionally, you can freeze, thaw, and preheat.

Nutrition: Calories: 45, Carbs: 8 g, Protein: 4 g, Fat: 1 g, Sugar: 6 g, Cholesterol: 1 mg

Chapter 6
Stage 3 Diet: Semi-Solid/Soft Foods

CHEESEBURGER SCRAMBLE

Preparation Time: 10 minutes
Cooking Time: 10 minutes
Servings: 4

Ingredients

- Nonstick cooking spray
- 8 ounces lean ground beef
- 4 large eggs
- ½ cup canned diced tomatoes, drained
- ½ cup shredded Cheddar cheese
- ¼ tsp salt

Directions

1. Spray your large skillet using cooking spray and cook the ground beef over medium heat for about 3 minutes, frequently stirring, until fully browned.
2. Remove the beef from the heat. Drain the fat into a bowl or jar for disposal, spoon the beef into a separate bowl or plate, and set it aside.
3. Put back your skillet over medium heat and spray again with cooking spray. Crack the eggs into a small bowl and beat well.
4. Pour the eggs into your skillet and cook for 2 to 3 minutes, frequently stirring, until the eggs are set.

5. Reduce the heat to low. Add the tomato, cheddar cheese, beef, and salt to the skillet and mix well, allowing the mixture to heat for 1 to 2 more minutes, or until the cheese is melted.
6. Remove from the heat and serve.

Nutrition: Calories: 218, Protein: 21 g, Fat: 13 g, Carbs: 2 g, Cholesterol: 6 mg

Cinnamon Protein Oatmeal

Preparation Time: 5 minutes

Cooking Time: 15 minutes

Servings: 4

Ingredients

- 1 cup quick-cooking oats
- 1 cup boiling water
- Stevia or Splenda to taste
- ¼ tsp salt
- ½ tsp ground cinnamon or more to taste
- ½ cup skim milk
- 2 scoops vanilla protein powder
- Zero calorie butter flavored cooking spray
- 2 tbsp sugar-free pancake syrup

Directions

1. Add oats, protein powder, sweetener, and milk into a microwave-safe bowl and stir until the mixture is thick but well combined and free from lumps.
2. Pour boiling water, about 2 to 3 tbsp at a time, and mix well each time. When all of the water is added, the mixture will be of pouring consistency.
3. Place the bowl in the microwave and cook for 2 minutes.
4. Stir in pancake syrup, salt, cinnamon, and some butter-flavored spray. Taste a bit of it and add more sweetener or cinnamon if desired.
5. Serve 1 portion in a bowl. Cool the remaining oatmeal, transfer it into an airtight container, and refrigerate for up to 3 days.

Nutrition: Calories: 218, Protein: 21 g, Fat: 13 g, Carbs: 2 g, Cholesterol: 11 mg

Deviled Egg and Bacon

Preparation Time: 10 minutes
Cooking Time: 0 minutes
Servings: 8
Ingredients

- 8 eggs, hard-boiled and peeled, halved lengthwise, yolk separated
- 3 tbsp no salt added chickpeas, rinsed and drained
- ½ cup low-fat plain Greek yogurt
- 1 tbsp Dijon mustard
- ¼ tsp paprika
- 2 slices bacon, cooked and crumbled
- 2 tbsp dill, chopped

Directions

1. Process the separated egg yolk in your food processor. Mix the chickpeas, Greek yogurt, Dijon mustard, and half of the dill with 1 tbsp of water.
2. Process in your food processor on and off until completely smooth. Trim the bottom of every white, so it rests flat before slicing a sliver off the bottom.
3. Place the ingredients in a bowl and stir until well mixed. Fill every egg white with the yolk mixture by spooning or piping it in.
4. Add paprika, bacon crumbles, and the last of the dill as needed. Serve!

Nutrition: Calories: 91, Carbs: 0 g, Fat: 7 g, Protein: 5 g, Cholesterol: 12 mg

Fluffy Egg White Omelet

Preparation Time: 10 minutes
Cooking Time: 10 minutes
Servings: 1

Ingredients

- 4 large egg whites
- ¼ tsp kosher salt
- ⅛ tsp freshly ground black pepper
- ⅛ tsp garlic powder
- 1 tbsp grated Parmesan cheese
- ¼ cup chopped scallions, green parts
- ⅓ cup firm cherry tomatoes halved
- Olive oil spray

Directions

1. Heat a nonstick 8-inch skillet for 2 to 3 minutes on medium heat.
2. Whip the egg whites, salt, pepper, and garlic powder in a medium bowl until frothy. Add the parmesan and mix well.
3. Fold in the green onions and tomatoes with a spatula. Spray the skillet lightly with olive oil spray, then add the egg whites and cook them while tilting the skillet.
4. Reduce the heat to medium-low after a few minutes. Serve immediately.

Nutrition: Calories: 210, Carbs: 2 g, Fat: 16 g, Protein: 15 g, Cholesterol: 23 mg

Brussels Sprouts

Preparation Time: 10 minutes
Cooking Time: 25 minutes
Servings: 4

Ingredients

- 8 ounces whole-wheat linguine
- ⅓ cup, plus 2 tbsp extra-virgin olive oil, divided
- 1 medium sweet onion, diced
- 2 to 3 garlic cloves, smashed
- 8 ounces Brussels sprouts, chopped
- ½ cup chicken stock, as needed
- ⅓ cup dry white wine
- ½ cup shredded Parmesan cheese
- 1 lemon, cut in quarters

Directions

1. Bring a large pot of water to a boil and cook the pasta according to the package directions. Drain, reserving 1 cup of pasta water. Mix the cooked pasta with 2 tbsp of olive oil, then set aside.
2. In a large sauté pan or skillet, heat the remaining ⅓ cup of olive oil on medium heat. Add the onion to the pan and cook for about 5 minutes, until softened. Add the smashed garlic cloves and cook for 1 minute, until fragrant.
3. Add the Brussels sprouts and cook covered for 15 minutes. Add chicken stock as needed to prevent burning. Once Brussels sprouts have wilted and are fork-tender, add white wine and cook down for about 7 minutes, until reduced.
4. Add the pasta to the skillet and add the pasta water as needed.

5   Serve with the Parmesan cheese and lemon for squeezing over the dish right before eating.

Nutrition: Calories: 530, Carbs: 95.4 g, Protein: 5.0 g, Fat: 16.5 g, Cholesterol: 7 mg

Pumpkin Pie Oatmeal

Preparation Time: 5 minutes
Cooking Time: 5 minutes
Servings: 4
Ingredients

- ⅔ cup old-fashioned oats
- ¼ tsp ground cinnamon
- ¼ tsp ground ginger
- ¼ tsp ground cloves
- 2 tsp Truvia baking blend
- 1 cup canned pumpkin
- 1 cup unsalted, 1% cottage cheese

Directions

1. Add oat, pumpkin, cinnamon, ginger, cloves, and Truvia into a microwave- safe bowl and stir. Cook on High in the microwave for 2 minutes. Stir after about 1 minute of cooking.
2. Add cottage cheese and stir. Cook for 60 to 80 seconds or until the oats are cooked.
3. Once it is cooked, let it rest for 2 to 4 minutes before serving.
4. Divide into 2 bowls. You can eat 1 bowl now and store the other in the refrigerator (keep it covered) for up to 3 to 4 days.

Nutrition: Calories: 218, Protein: 21 g, Fat: 13 g, Carbs: 2 g, Cholesterol: 7 mg

Rustic Vegetable and Brown Rice Bowl

Preparation Time: 15 minutes
Cooking Time: 10 minutes
Servings: 4
Ingredients

- Nonstick cooking spray
- 2 cups broccoli florets
- 2 cups cauliflower florets
- 1 (15-ounce) can chickpeas, drained and rinsed
- 1 cup carrots sliced 1 inch thick
- 2 to 3 tbsp extra-virgin olive oil, divided
- Salt
- Freshly ground black pepper
- 2 cups cooked brown rice

For the Dressing

- 3 to 4 tbsp tahini
- 2 tbsp honey
- 1 lemon, juiced
- 1 garlic clove, minced
- Salt
- Freshly ground black pepper

Directions

1. Turn on the oven to 400°F. Apply cooking spray to 2 baking sheets.
2. Spread the broccoli and cauliflower on the first baking sheet and the chickpeas and carrots on the second. Before putting

the sheets in the oven, toss each one with half the oil and some salt and pepper.

3. Cook the broccoli and cauliflower for 20 minutes or until soft, together with the carrots and chickpeas, leaving the carrots barely crunchy. Halfway through cooking, stir each.
4. To make the dressing, combine the tahini, honey, lemon juice, salt, and garlic in a bowl.
5. Spoon the rice into individual bowls, top with a layer of vegetables, then add the dressing.

Nutrition: Calories: 192, Carbs: 12.7 g, Protein: 3.8 g, Fat: 15.5 g, Cholesterol: 8 mg

Smoked Mackerel Scrambled Eggs

Preparation Time: 5 minutes

Cooking Time: 10 minutes

Servings: 4

Ingredients

- 3 large eggs
- ½ ounce reduced-fat butter spread
- Sea salt to taste
- Freshly ground pepper to taste
- Chopped chives to garnish
- 2 tbsp nonfat milk
- 1 peppered smoked mackerel filet, flaked
- 2 whole-wheat bagels, split

Directions

1. Crack the eggs into a bowl. Add milk, salt, and pepper, and whisk well.
2. Add reduced-fat butter spread into a nonstick pan and let it melt over medium heat.
3. Add egg mixture and stir every now and then until the eggs are slightly cooked.
4. Add mackerel into the pan and mix well. Cook until the eggs are soft- cooked. Stir often.
5. Turn off the heat and serve.
6. For phase 4, toast the bagels to the desired doneness.
7. Top the bagels with scrambled eggs.
8. Garnish with chives and serve.

Nutrition: Calories: 218, Protein: 21 g, Fat: 13 g, Carbs: 2 g, Cholesterol: 6 mg

Tasty Avocado Sauce Over Zoodles

Preparation Time: 10 minutes

Cooking Time: 0 minutes

Servings: 2

Ingredients

- 1 zucchini peeled and spiralized into noodles
- 4 tbsp pine nuts
- 2 tbsp lemon juice
- 1 avocado peeled and pitted
- 12 sliced cherry tomatoes
- ⅓ cup water
- 1 ¼ cup basil
- Pepper and salt to taste

Directions

1. Make the sauce in a blender by adding pine nuts, lemon juice, avocado, water, and basil. Pulse until smooth and creamy. Season with pepper and salt to taste. Mix well.
2. Place zoodles in a salad bowl. Pour over the avocado sauce and toss well to coat.
3. Add cherry tomatoes, serve, and enjoy.

Nutrition: Calories: 313, Protein: 6.8 g, Carbs: 18.7 g, Fat: 26.8 g, Cholesterol: 5 mg

Veggie Ramen Miso Soup

Preparation Time: 5 minutes
Cooking Time: 15 minutes
Servings: 1
Ingredients

- 2 tsp thinly sliced green onion
- A pinch of salt
- ½ tsp shoyu
- 2 tbsp mellow white miso
- 1 cup zucchini, cut into angel hair spirals
- ½ cup thinly sliced cremini mushrooms
- ½ medium carrot, cut into angel hair spirals
- ½ cup baby spinach leaves – optional
- 2 ¼ cups water
- ½ box medium firm tofu, cut into ¼-inch cubes
- 1 hardboiled egg

Directions

1. In a small bowl, mix ¼ cup of water and miso. Set aside.
2. In a small saucepan on medium-high fire, bring to a boil 2 cups water, mushrooms, tofu, and carrots. Add salt, shoyu, and miso mixture. Allow boiling for 5 minutes. Remove from fire and add green onion, zucchini, and baby spinach leaves if using.
3. Let soup stand for 5 minutes before transferring it to individual bowls. Garnish with ½ of a hardboiled egg per bowl, serve and enjoy.

Nutrition: Calories: 335, Carbs: 19.0 g, Protein: 30.6 g, Fat: 17.6 g, Cholesterol: 5 mg

Chapter 7
Stage 4 Diet: Breakfast Recipes

ALMONDS BREAKFAST SALAD

Preparation Time: 10 minutes
Cooking Time: 20 minutes
Servings: 4
Ingredients

- 4 whole eggs
- 2 cups cherry tomatoes or heirloom tomatoes cut in half or wedges
- 10 cups arugula
- A ½ chopped seedless cucumber
- 1 large avocado
- 1 cup cooked or cooled quinoa
- ½ cup chopped mixed herbs like dill and mint
- 1 cup chopped Almonds
- 1 lemon
- Extra virgin olive oil
- Sea salt
- Freshly ground black pepper

Directions

1. In this recipe, the eggs are the first thing that needs to be cooked. Start with soft boiling the eggs. To do that, you need to get water in a pan and let it sit to boil. Once it starts boiling, reduce the heat to simmer and lower the eggs into the water and let them cook for about 6 minutes. After they are boiled, wash the eggs with cold water and set them aside.

Peel them when they are cool and ready to use.

2. Combine quinoa, arugula, cucumbers, and tomatoes in a bowl and add a little bit of olive oil over the top. Toss it with salt and pepper to equally season all of it.
3. Once all that is done, serve the salad on 4 plates and garnish it with sliced
4. avocados and halved eggs. After that, season it with some more pepper and salt.
5. To top it all off, then use almonds and sprinkle some herbs along with some lemon zest and olive oil.

Nutrition: Calories: 85, Protein: 3.4 g, Fat: 3.46 g, Carbs: 6.71, Cholesterol: 78 mg

Smoked Salmon and Poached Eggs on Toast

Preparation Time: 10 minutes
Cooking Time: 10 minutes
Servings: 4
Ingredients

- 2 oz avocado smashed
- 2 slices bread toasted
- A pinch of kosher salt and cracked black pepper
- ¼ tsp freshly squeezed lemon juice
- 2 eggs, poached
- 4 oz smoked salmon
- 1 tbsp thinly sliced scallions
- Splash Kikkoman soy sauce optional
- Microgreens are optional

Directions

1. Take a small bowl and then smash the avocado into it. Then, add the lemon juice and also a pinch of salt to the mixture. Then, mix it well and set it aside.
2. After that, poach the eggs and toast the bread for some time.
3. Once the bread is toasted, you will have to spread the avocado on both slices and after that, add the smoked salmon to each slice.
4. Thereafter, carefully transfer the poached eggs to the respective toasts.
5. Add a splash of Kikkoman soy sauce and some cracked pepper; then, just garnish with scallions and microgreens.

Nutrition: Calories: 459, Protein: 31 g, Fat: 22 g, Carbs: 33 g, Cholesterol: 81 mg

Honey Almond Ricotta Spread With Peaches

Preparation Time: 5 minutes

Cooking Time: 10 minutes

Servings: 4

Ingredients

- ½ cup fisher sliced almonds
- 1 cup whole milk ricotta
- ¼ tsp almond extract
- Zest from an orange, optional
- 1 tsp honey
- Sliced peaches
- Extra honey for drizzling

Directions

1. Cut peaches into a proper shape and then brush them with olive oil. After that, set it aside.
2. Take a bowl; combine the ingredients for the filling. Set aside.
3. Then just pre-heat the grill to medium.
4. Place peaches cut side down onto the greased grill.
5. Close the lid cover and then just grill until the peaches have softened, approximately 6 to 10 minutes, depending on the size of the peaches.
6. Then you will have to place peach halves onto a serving plate.
7. Put a spoon of about 1 tbsp of ricotta mixture into the cavity (you are also allowed to use a small scooper).
8. Sprinkle it with slivered almonds and honey.

9   Decorate with mint leaves.

Nutrition: Calories: 187, Protein: 7g, Fat: 9g, Carbs: 18g, Cholesterol: 40 mg

Pastry-Less Spanakopita

Preparation Time: 5minutes

Cooking Time: 20minutes

Servings: 4

Ingredients

- ⅛ tsp black pepper, add as per taste
- ⅓ cup extra virgin olive oil
- 4 lightly beaten eggs
- 7 cups Lettuce, preferably a spring mix (mesclun)
- ½ cup crumbled Feta cheese
- ⅛ tsp Sea salt, add to taste
- 1 finely chopped medium Yellow onion

Directions

1. For this delicious recipe, you need to first start by preheating the oven to 180°C and grease the flan dish.
2. Once done, pour the extra virgin olive oil into a large saucepan and heat it over medium heat with the onions, until they are translucent. To that, add greens and keep stirring until all the ingredients are wilted.
3. After completing that, you should season it with salt and pepper and transfer the greens to the prepared dish and sprinkle on some feta cheese.
4. Pour the eggs and bake them for 20 minutes till it is cooked through and slightly brown.

Nutrition: Calories: 325, Protein: 11.2 g, Fat: 27.9 g, Carbs: 7.3 g, Cholesterol: 67 mg

Date and Walnut Overnight Oats

Preparation Time: 5 minutes

Cooking Time: 0 minutes

Servings: 2

Ingredients

- ¼ cup Greek yogurt, plain
- ⅓ cup yogurt
- ⅔ cup oats
- 1 cup milk
- 2 tsp date syrup or you can also use maple syrup or honey
- 1 mashed banana
- ¼ tsp cinnamon
- ¼ cup walnuts
- A pinch of salt (approx. ⅛ tsp)

Directions

1. Firstly, get a mason jar or a small bowl and add all the ingredients.
2. After that stir and mix all the ingredients well.
3. Cover it securely, and cool it in a refrigerator overnight.
4. After that, take it out the next morning, add more liquid or cinnamon if required, and serve cold. (However, you can also microwave it for people with a warmer palate.)

Nutrition: Calories: 350, Protein: 14 g, Fat: 12 g, Carbs: 49 g, Cholesterol: 68 mg

Greek Quinoa Breakfast Bowl

Preparation Time: 10 minutes
Cooking Time: 20 minutes
Servings: 2
Ingredients
- 2 large eggs
- ¾ cup Greek yogurt
- 2 cups cooked quinoa
- ¾ cup muhammara
- 3 oz baby spinach
- 4 oz marinated kalamata olives
- 6 oz sliced cherry tomatoes
- 1 halved lemon
- Hot chili oil
- Salt & pepper to taste
- Fresh dill and sesame seeds to garnish

Directions
1. Add all the ingredients, Greek yogurt, granulated garlic, onion powder, salt, and pepper, whisk them all together and set aside.
2. In a different large saucepan, heat the olive oil on medium-high heat and add the spinach. You have to keep in mind to cook the spinach till it is slightly wilted. This takes about 3 to 4 minutes.
3. After that, cook the cherry tomatoes in the same skillet for 3 to 4 minutes till they are softened.
4. Stir in the egg mixture into this for about 7 to 9 minutes, until it has set and cooked so that they get scrambled.

5   After the eggs have set, stir in the quinoa and feta and cook until it is heated all the way through and serve it hot with some fresh dill and sesame seeds to garnish.

Nutrition: Calories: 357, Protein: 23 g, Fat: 20 g, Carbs: 20 g, Cholesterol: 54 mg

Honey-Caramelized Figs With Greek Yogurt

Preparation Time: 5 minutes

Cooking Time: 5 minutes

Servings: 4

Ingredients

- 4 fresh halved figs
- 2 tbsp melted butter, 30ml
- 2 tbsp brown sugar, 30ml
- 2 cups Greek yogurt 500ml
- ¼ cup honey, 60ml

Directions

1. Take a non-stick skillet and preheat it over a medium flame
2. Put the butter on the pan and toss the figs into it and sprinkle some brown sugar over it.
3. Put the figs on the pan and cut off the side of the figs.
4. Cook the figs on a medium flame for 2 to 3 minutes until they turn golden brown.
5. Turn over the figs and cook them for 2 to 3 minutes again
6. Remove the figs from the pan and let it cool down a little.
7. Take a plate and put a scoop of Greek yogurt on it. Put the cooked figs over the yogurts and drizzle the honey over it

Nutrition: Calories: 350, Protein: 6 g, Fat: 19 g, Carbs: 40 g, Cholesterol: 67 mg

Savory Quinoa Egg Muffins With Spinach

Preparation Time: 15 minutes
Cooking Time: 20 minutes
Servings: 2
Ingredients

- 1 cup quinoa
- 2 cups water
- 4 oz spinach which is about 1 cup
- ½ chopped onion
- 2 whole eggs
- ¼ cup grated cheese
- ½ tsp oregano or thyme
- ½ tsp garlic powder
- ½ tsp salt

Directions

1. Take a medium saucepan and put water in it. Add the quinoa to the water and bring the whole thing to a simmer. Cover the pan and cook it for 10 minutes till the water gets absorbed by the quinoa. Remove the saucepan from the heat and let it cool down.
2. Take a nonstick pan and heat the onions till they turn soft and then add spinach. Cook all of them together till the spinach gets a little wilted and then remove it from the heat.
3. Preheat the oven to 176.667 C
4. Take a muffin pan and grease it lightly
5. Take a large bowl and add the cooked quinoa along with the cooked onions, spinach, and add cheese, eggs, thyme or oregano, salt, garlic powder, pepper and mix them together.

6. Put a spoonful of the mixture into a muffin tin. Make sure it is ¼ of a cup.
7. In the preheated pan, put it in the pan and bake it for around 20 minutes.

Nutrition: Calories: 61, Protein: 4 g, Fat: 3 g, Carbs: 6 g, Cholesterol: 54 mg

Avocado Tomato Gouda Socca Pizza

Preparation Time: 20 minutes
Cooking Time: 20 minutes
Servings: 2
Ingredients

- 1¼ cups chickpea or garbanzo bean flour
- 1¼ cups cold water
- 1tsp avocado or olive oil. Take 1 tsp extra for heating the pan
- 1 tsp Onion powder/other herb seasoning powder
- 10 to 12-inch cast iron pan
- 1 sliced tomato
- ½ avocado
- 2oz thinly sliced Gouda
- ¼ cup Tomato sauce
- 3 tsp chopped green scallion/onion
- Sprouted greens
- Extra pepper/salt for sprinkling on top of the pizza

Directions

1. Mix the flour with 2 tsp of olive oil, herbs, water, and whisk it until a smooth mixture forms. Keep it at room temperature for around 15 to 20 minutes to let the batter settle
2. In the meantime, preheat the oven and place the pan inside the oven and let it get heated for around 10 minutes
3. When the pan gets preheated, chop up the vegetables into fine slices
4. Remove the pan after 10 minutes using oven mitts
5. Put 1 tsp of oil and swirl it all around to coat the pan
6. Pour the batter into the pan and tilt the pan so that the batter

spreads evenly throughout the pan.

7. Turn down the over to 425°F and place back the pan for 5 to 8 minutes
8. Remove the pan from the oven and add the sliced avocado, tomato and on top of that, add the gouda slices and the onion slices
9. Put the pizza back into the oven and wait till the cheese get melted or the sides of the bread get crusty and brown
10. Remove the pizza from the pan and add the microgreens on top, along with the toppings.

Nutrition: Calories: 416, Protein: 15 g, Fat: 10 g, Carbs: 37 g, Cholesterol: 98 mg

Sunny-Side Up Baked Eggs With Swiss Chard, Feta, and Basil

Preparation Time: 15 minutes

Cooking Time: 10 minutes

Servings: 4

Ingredients

- 2 bell peppers, any color
- 1 tbsp extra-virgin olive oil
- 8 large eggs
- ¾ tsp kosher salt, divided
- ¼ tsp freshly ground black pepper, divided
- 1 avocado, peeled, pitted, and diced
- ¼ cup red onion, diced
- ¼ cup fresh basil, chopped
- Juice ½ lime

Directions

1. Remove the peppers' stems and seeds. From each pepper, cut 2 rings that are 2 inches thick. Set aside the remaining bell pepper after chopping it into small pieces.

2. In a big skillet over medium heat, warm the olive oil. Place 1 egg in the center of each ring of 4 bell peppers after adding them. Add ⅛ tsp of black pepper and ¼ tsp of salt to season. Cook for 2 to 3 minutes, or until the egg whites are mostly set but the yolks are still runny. For over easy, gently turn after 1 minute of cooking. Repeat with the remaining 4 bell pepper rings after transferring the egg-bell pepper rings to a platter or plates.

3. Combine the avocado, onion, basil, and saved lime juice in a medium bowl.

Nutrition: Calories: 270, Protein: 15 g, Fat: 19 g, Carbs: 12 g, Cholesterol: 87 mg

Tomato and Lentils Salad

Preparation Time: 10 minutes
Cooking Time: 35 minutes
Servings: 4

Ingredients

- 2 yellow onions, chopped
- 4 garlic cloves, minced
- 2 cups brown lentils
- 1 tbsp olive oil
- A pinch of salt and black pepper
- ½ tsp sweet paprika
- ½ tsp ginger, grated
- 3 cups water
- ¼ cup lemon juice
- ¾ cup Greek yogurt
- 3 tbsp tomato paste

Directions

1. Heat up a pot with the oil over medium-high heat, add the onions and sauté for 2 minutes.
2. Add the garlic and the lentils, stir and cook for 1 minute more.
3. Add the water, bring to a simmer and cook covered for 30 minutes.
4. Add the lemon juice and the remaining ingredients except for the yogurt. Toss, and divide the mix into bowls, top with the yogurt and serve.

Nutrition: Calories: 294, Fat: 3.5 g, Fiber: 9.6 g, Carbs: 26.6 g, Protein: 15.4 g, Cholesterol: 8 mg

Egg and Arugula Salad

Preparation Time: 15 minutes
Cooking Time: 5 minutes
Servings: 4
Ingredients

- 3 tomatoes
- 1 cucumber
- 4 eggs, boiled, peeled
- ½ cup black olives pitted
- ¼ red onion, peeled
- ½ cup arugula
- ⅓ cup Plain yogurt
- 1 tsp lemon juice
- ¼ tsp paprika
- ⅓ tsp sea salt
- ½ tsp dried oregano

Directions

1. Chop tomatoes and cucumber into medium cubes and transfer to the salad bowl.
2. Then tear the arugula and add it to the salad bowl.
3. In the shallow bowl whisk together Plain yogurt, lemon juice, paprika, sea salt, and dried oregano.
4. Chop the boiled eggs roughly and add them to the salad.
5. Add black olives (slice them if desired).
6. Then add red onion.
7. Shake the salad well.

8   Pour Plain yogurt dressing over the salad and stir it only before serving.

Nutrition: Calories: 169, Fat: 6.5 g, Fiber: 2.6 g, Carbs: 10.6 g, Protein: 9.4 g, Cholesterol: 89 mg

Fruit Packed Breakfast Wrap

Preparation Time: 10 minutes

Cooking Time: 0 minutes

Servings: 1

Ingredients

- 1 tortilla, whole wheat variety
- 3 tbsp ricotta cheese, regular variety
- 1 tbsp jelly, strawberry flavored and low in sugar
- ⅓ cup strawberries, fresh and thinly sliced

Directions

1. Spread your ricotta cheese and jelly on your tortilla.
2. Sprinkle your strawberries over your cheese and jelly. Roll up your tortilla burrito-style and enjoy it right away.

Nutrition: Calories: 301, Carbs: 33 g, Fat: 8 g, Protein: 28 g, Cholesterol: 90 mg

Baked Ricotta Florentine

Preparation Time: 10 minutes
Cooking Time: 20 minutes
Servings: 4
Ingredients

- Olive oil spray extra virgin
- ¼ cup fresh spinach, chopped finely
- 2 tbsp minced sun-dried tomatoes
- 8 oz. Ricotta cheese total fat or part-skim
- ½ cup shredded mozzarella cheese
- 2 tbsp grated Parmesan cheese
- ½ cup mushrooms

Directions

1. Set the oven to 350°F.
2. Cover the insides of your ramekins with olive oil. Heat a medium-sized sauté pan with a spray of olive oil.
3. Sauté the chopped spinach until it has wilted in a skillet over medium heat.
4. Mix the ricotta, mozzarella, parmesan, spinach, and sun-dried tomatoes in a medium bowl.
5. Divide the mixture evenly in your prepared ramekins, and add more shredded mozzarella to every ramekin.
6. Bake for 15 to 20 minutes in the oven or until the cheese has melted. Serve!

Nutrition: Calories: 158, Protein: 11g, Fat:7g, Carbs: 3g, Cholesterol: 65 mg

Chicken With Spinach and Tomato

Preparation Time: 10 minutes
Cooking Time: 20 minutes
Servings: 6

Ingredients

- 2 ½ lb Chicken breast (skinless boneless) cut into 1" pieces
- 2 tbsp olive oil
- Salt, as needed
- 2 cloves garlic minced
- Ground black pepper, as needed
- 7 oz. Baby spinach
- 15 oz. canned diced tomatoes
- Grated parmesan cheese (optional)

Directions

1. Place your big saucepan over medium heat and coat it with olive oil. Add the garlic and chicken to the heated oil—season with salt and pepper to taste.
2. Add the spinach, tomatoes, and mushrooms when the pinkish shade of chicken and the fluids run clear.
3. Cook till the liquid has been reduced to roughly half its original volume. If necessary, season the dish. If preferred, top with cheese right before serving.

Nutrition: Calories: 173, Carbs: 11 g, Protein: 40 g, Fats: 6 g, Cholesterol: 33 mg

Egg White "Pizza"

Preparation Time: 5 minutes
Cooking Time: 5 minutes
Servings: 4
Ingredients

- 1 tbsp extra-virgin olive oil
- 12 large egg whites (1 ½ cups egg whites)
- ½ tsp Italian seasoning
- ½ tsp garlic powder
- ¼ tsp salt
- Nonstick cooking spray (optional)
- ½ cup shredded mozzarella cheese
- 1 cup sliced tomato (1 large tomato)

Directions

1. In your large skillet, heat the oil over medium heat.
2. Beat the egg whites with the Italian seasoning, garlic powder, and salt in a large bowl.
3. Pour the mixture into the skillet and cover with a lid—Cook for 1 to 2 minutes, or until egg whites start to bubble.
4. Use a spatula to carefully lift at the edges to ensure the egg whites are not sticking to the skillet.
5. Remove the lid, then sprinkle the mozzarella cheese over the eggs. Place the tomato slices on top. Cover and heat for another 1 or 2 minutes until the cheese melts.
6. Carefully remove the egg white pizza from the pan. Divide into quarters and serve hot.

Nutrition: Calories: 180, Carbs: 6 g, Protein: 19 g, Fat: 11 g, Cholesterol: 87 mg

Greek Yogurt Breakfast Parfait

Preparation Time: 10 minutes + chilling time
Cooking Time: 0 minutes
Servings: 8
Ingredients

- 4 cups nonfat plain Greek yogurt
- 1 cup sucralose granules
- 1 ½ tsp vanilla extract
- 2 cups granola cereal
- 8 cups frozen mixed fruit, no sugar added

Directions

1. Pour the yogurt, sweetener, and vanilla extract into a large mixing bowl and stir until well blended.
2. Fill each of the 8 plastic glasses with 1 cup of frozen fruit. Refrigerate until ready to use.
3. Before serving, sprinkle ¼ cup granola over the top.

Nutrition: Calories: 190, Carbs: 2g, Fat: 7g, Protein: 26g, Cholesterol: 88 mg

Italian-Style Scramble

Preparation Time: 5 minutes
Cooking Time: 5 minutes
Servings: 4
Ingredients

- Nonstick cooking spray
- 8 large eggs
- 1 cup canned diced tomatoes, drained
- 1 cup shredded mozzarella cheese
- 1 tsp Italian seasoning
- 1 tsp garlic powder
- ¼ tsp salt

Directions

1. Spray your large skillet with nonstick cooking spray and heat over medium heat.
2. In a large bowl, combine the eggs, tomato, mozzarella cheese, Italian seasoning, garlic powder, and salt, and beat well until combined.
3. Pour the mixture into your skillet and cook for 3 to 5 minutes, frequently stirring, until the eggs are set. Remove from the heat and serve.

Nutrition: Calories: 241, Protein: 21 g, Fat: 16 g, Carbs: 6 g, Cholesterol: 147 mg

Shrimp Toast–Style Seafood Cakes

Preparation Time: 10 minutes

Cooking Time: 15 minutes

Servings: 8

Ingredients

- ½ cup canned baby shrimp
- 4 tbsp almond flour
- 2 tbsp coconut aminos, plus more for dipping
- 2 tbsp unsweetened almond milk
- 1 large egg
- ½ tsp garlic powder
- ½ tsp ginger powder
- ½ tsp chopped parsley or dried
- ¼ tsp salt
- 1 tbsp extra-virgin olive oil
- ⅓ cup finely diced yellow onion
- Nonstick cooking spray (optional)

Directions

1. Combine the shrimp, almond flour, coconut aminos, almond milk, egg, garlic powder, ginger powder, parsley, and salt in your large mixing bowl. Mix well and set aside.
2. In your medium skillet, heat the oil over medium heat. Cook the onion for about 5 minutes or until slightly translucent.
3. Remove and add to the shrimp mixture. Incorporate well.
4. Scoop a heaping tbsp of your shrimp mixture into the same skillet and flatten with the back of a spoon. Repeat with the remaining shrimp mixture to make 8 cakes.

5. Cook the shrimp cakes for 3 to 4 minutes on each side, or until each side is a little more than golden brown, working in batches if needed.
6. Remove the cakes from the heat and enjoy with additional coconut aminos on the side for dipping.

Nutrition: Calories: 124, Protein: 7 g, Fat: 9g, Carbs: 5 g, Cholesterol: 100 mg

Chapter 8
Meat and Seafood Recipes

LAMB STEW

Preparation Time: 10 minutes
Cooking Time: 8 hours
Servings: 2
Ingredients

- ½ lb lamb, boneless and cubed
- ¼ cup green olives, sliced
- 2 tbsp lemon juice
- ½ onion, chopped
- 1 garlic cloves, minced
- 2 fresh thyme sprigs
- ¼ tsp turmeric
- ½ tsp pepper
- ¼ tsp salt

Directions

1. Fill the crock pot with all the ingredients and stir well.
2. Cook on low for 8 hours while covered. Stir thoroughly, then plate.

Nutrition: Calories: 297, Fat: 20.3 g, Carbs: 5.4 g, Sugar: 1.5 g, Protein: 21 g, Cholesterol: 80 mg

Flavorful Beef Stew

Preparation Time: 10 minutes
Cooking Time: 2 hours 10 minutes
Servings: 4

Ingredients

- 2 lb beef chuck, diced into chunks
- 3 thyme sprigs
- 2 bay leaves
- 2 oz olives, pitted
- 3 cups red wine
- 2 garlic cloves, chopped
- 2 tbsp olive oil
- Pepper
- Salt

Directions

1. Season meat with pepper and salt.
2. Heat oil in a pan over high heat.
3. Add meat in hot oil and sear for 3 to 4 minutes on each side.
4. Add bay leaves, half-red wine, garlic, and thyme. Bring to a boil, turn the heat to low and simmer for 90 minutes. Remove pan from heat.
5. Add olives and the remaining red wine. Stir well.
6. Return the pan to the heat and simmer for 30 minutes more.
7. Serve hot and enjoy.

Nutrition: Calories: 630, Fat: 20.3 g, Carbs: 7 g, Sugar: 1.4 g, Protein: 69.2 g, Cholesterol: 203 mg

Herb Ground Beef

Preparation Time: 10 minutes

Cooking Time: 15 minutes

Servings: 4

Ingredients

- 1 lb ground beef
- ½ tsp dried parsley
- ½ tsp dried basil
- ½ tsp dried oregano
- 1 tsp garlic, minced
- 1 tbsp olive oil
- 1 tsp pepper
- ¼ tsp nutmeg
- ½ tsp dried thyme
- ½ tsp dried rosemary
- 1 tsp salt

Directions

1. Heat oil in a pan over medium heat.
2. Add ground meat to the pan and fry until cooked.
3. Add remaining ingredients and stir well.
4. Serve and enjoy.

Nutrition: Calories: 215, Fat: 7.2 g, Carbs: 1 g, Sugar: 0.2 g, Protein: 34 g, Cholesterol: 101 mg

Olive Feta Beef

Preparation Time: 10 minutes
Cooking Time: 6 hours
Servings: 8
Ingredients

- 2 lb beef stew meat, cut into half-inch pieces
- 1 cup olives, pitted and cut in half
- 30 oz can tomatoes, diced
- ½ cup feta cheese, crumbled
- ¼ tsp pepper
- ½ tsp salt

Directions

1. Fill the crock pot with all the ingredients and stir well.
2. Cover and cook for 6 hours on high.
3. Add salt and pepper to taste.
4. Stir well, then plate.

Nutrition: Calories: 370, Fat: 14 g, Carbs: 9 g, Sugar: 5.3 g, Protein: 49.1 g, Cholesterol: 8 mg

Italian Beef Casserole

Preparation Time: 10 minutes
Cooking Time: 1 hour 30 minutes
Servings: 6
Ingredients

- 1 lb lean stew beef, cut into chunks
- 3 tsp paprika
- 4 oz black olives, sliced
- 7 oz can tomatoes, chopped
- 1 tbsp tomato puree
- ¼ tsp garlic powder
- 2 tsp herb de Provence
- 2 cups beef stock
- 2 tbsp olive oil

Directions

1. Preheat the oven to 350°F.
2. Heat oil in a pan over medium heat.
3. Add meat to the pan and cook until brown.
4. Add stock, olives, tomatoes, tomato puree, garlic powder, herb de Provence, and paprika. Stir well and bring to a boil.
5. Transfer the meat mixture to the casserole dish.
6. Cover and cook in preheated oven for 1 hour and 30 minutes.
7. Serve and enjoy.

Nutrition: Calories: 228, Fat: 11.6 g, Carbs: 6 g, Sugar: 1.4 g, Protein: 26 g, Cholesterol: 11 mg

Roasted Sirloin Steak

Preparation Time: 10 minutes
Cooking Time: 30 minutes
Servings: 6
Ingredients

- 2 lb sirloin steak, cut into 1" cubes
- 2 garlic cloves, minced
- 3 tbsp fresh lemon juice
- 1 tsp dried oregano
- ¼ cup water
- ¼ cup olive oil
- 2 cups fresh parsley, chopped
- ½ tsp pepper
- 1 tsp salt

Directions

1. Add all ingredients except beef into the large bowl and mix well.
2. Pour the bowl mixture into the large zip-lock bag.
3. Add beef to the bag and shake well and refrigerate for 1 hour.
4. Preheat the oven to 400°F.
5. Place marinated beef on a baking tray and bake in preheated oven for 30 minutes.
6. Serve and enjoy.

Nutrition: Calories: 365, Fat: 18.1 g, Carbs: 2 g, Sugar: 0.4 g, Protein: 46.6 g, Cholesterol: 135 mg

Easy Pork Kabobs

Preparation Time: 10 minutes
Cooking Time: 10 minutes
Servings: 6
Ingredients

- 2 lb pork tenderloin, cut into 1-inch cubes
- 1 onion, chopped
- ½ cup olive oil
- ½ cup red wine vinegar
- 2 tbsp fresh parsley, chopped
- 2 garlic cloves, chopped
- Pepper
- Salt

Directions

1. In a large zip-lock bag, mix together red wine vinegar, parsley, garlic, onion, and oil.
2. Add meat to the bag and marinate in the refrigerator overnight.
3. Remove marinated pork from the refrigerator and thread it onto soaked wooden skewers. Season with pepper and salt.
4. Preheat the grill over high heat.
5. Grill pork for 3 to 4 minutes on each side.
6. Serve and enjoy.

Nutrition: Calories: 375, Fat: 22 g, Carbs: 2.5 g, Sugar: 1 g, Protein: 40 g, Cholesterol: 110 mg

Tasty Meatballs

Preparation Time: 10 minutes
Cooking Time: 4 hours
Servings: 6

Ingredients

- 1 egg
- 2 tbsp fresh parsley, chopped
- 1 garlic clove, minced
- ½ lb ground beef
- ½ lb ground pork
- 14 oz can tomatoes, crushed
- 2 tbsp fresh basil, chopped
- ¼ tsp pepper
- ½ tsp salt

Directions

1. In a mixing bowl, mix together beef, pork, egg, parsley, garlic, pepper, and salt until well combined.
2. Make small balls from the meat mixture.
3. Arrange meatballs in the slow cooker.
4. Pour crushed tomatoes, basil, pepper, and salt over the meatballs.
5. Cover and cook on low for 4 hours.
6. Serve and enjoy.

Nutrition: Calories: 150, Fat: 4 g, Carbs: 4 g, Sugar: 2 g, Protein: 24 g, Cholesterol: 90 mg

97. Baked Patties

Preparation Time: 10 minutes
Cooking Time: 15 minutes
Servings: 4
Ingredients
- 1 lb ground lamb
- 1 tsp ground coriander
- 1 tsp ground cumin
- ¼ cup fresh parsley, chopped
- ¼ cup onion, minced
- ¼ tsp cayenne pepper
- ½ tsp ground allspice
- 1 tsp ground cinnamon
- 1 tbsp garlic, minced
- ¼ tsp pepper
- 1 tsp kosher salt

Directions
1. Preheat the oven to 450°C.
2. Add all ingredients into the large bowl and mix until well combined.
3. Make small balls from the meat mixture and place them on a baking tray and lightly flatten the meatballs with the back of the spoon.
4. Bake in preheated oven for 12 to 15 minutes.
5. Serve and enjoy.

Nutrition: Calories: 112, Fat: 4.3 g, Carbs: 1.3 g, Sugar: 0.2 g, Protein: 16 g, Cholesterol: 51 mg

Basil Cheese Pork Roast

Preparation Time: 10 minutes
Cooking Time: 6 hours
Servings: 8
Ingredients
- 2 lb lean pork roast, boneless
- 1 tsp garlic powder
- 1 tbsp parsley
- ½ cup cheddar cheese, grated
- 30 oz can tomatoes, diced
- 1 tsp dried oregano
- 1 tsp dried basil
- Pepper
- Salt

Directions
1. Add the meat to the crock pot.
2. Mix tomatoes, oregano, basil, garlic powder, parsley, cheese, pepper, and salt and pour over meat.
3. Cover and cook on low for 6 hours.
4. Serve and enjoy.

Nutrition: Calories: 260, Fat: 9 g, Carbs: 5.5 g, Sugar: 3.5 g, Protein: 35 g, Cholesterol: 97 mg

Beef Stroganoff

Preparation Time: 10 minutes

Cooking Time: 8 hours

Servings: 2

Ingredients

- ½ lb beef stew meat
- 10 oz mushroom soup, homemade
- 1 medium onion, chopped
- ½ cup sour cream
- 5 oz mushrooms, sliced
- Pepper and salt

Directions

1. Add all ingredients except sour cream into the crock pot and mix well.
2. Cover and cook on low for 8 hours.
3. Add sour cream and stir well.
4. Serve and enjoy.

Nutrition: Calories: 470, Fat: 25 g, Carbs: 8.6 g, Sugar: 3 g, Protein: 49 g, Cholesterol: 108 mg

Feta Lamb Patties

Preparation Time: 10 minutes

Cooking Time: 12 minutes

Servings: 4

Ingredients

- 1 lb ground lamb
- ½ tsp garlic powder
- ½ cup feta cheese, crumbled
- ¼ cup mint leaves, chopped
- ¼ cup roasted red pepper, chopped
- ¼ cup onion, chopped
- Pepper
- Salt

Directions

1. Add all ingredients into the bowl and mix until well combined.
2. Spray pan with cooking spray and heat over medium-high heat.
3. Make small patties from the meat mixture and place them on a hot pan and cook for 6 to 7 minutes on each side.
4. Serve and enjoy.

Nutrition: Calories: 270, Fat: 12 g, Carbs: 2.9 g, Sugar: 1.7 g, Protein: 34.9, Cholesterol: 89 mg

Greek Beef Roast

Preparation Time: 10 minutes
Cooking Time: 8 hours
Servings: 6
Ingredients

- 2 lb lean top round beef roast
- 1 tbsp Italian seasoning
- 6 garlic cloves, minced
- 1 onion, sliced
- 2 cups beef broth
- ½ cup red wine
- 1 tsp red pepper flakes
- Pepper
- Salt

Directions

1. Season meat with pepper and salt and place into the crock pot.
2. Pour the remaining ingredients over the meat.
3. Cover and cook on low for 8 hours.
4. Shred the meat using a fork.
5. Serve and enjoy.

Nutrition: Calories: 231, Fat: 6 g, Carbs: 4 g, Sugar: 1.4 g, Protein: 35 g, Cholesterol: 75 mg

Greek Pork Chops

Preparation Time: 10 minutes
Cooking Time: 8 minutes
Servings: 8

Ingredients

- 8 pork chops, boneless
- 4 tsp dried oregano
- 2 tbsp Worcestershire sauce
- 3 tbsp fresh lemon juice
- ¼ cup olive oil
- 1 tsp ground mustard
- 2 tsp garlic powder
- 2 tsp onion powder
- Pepper
- Salt

Directions

1. Whisk together oil, garlic powder, onion powder, oregano, Worcestershire sauce, lemon juice, mustard, pepper, and salt.
2. Place pork chops in a baking dish then pour marinade over pork chops and coat well. Place in refrigerator overnight.
3. Preheat the grill.
4. Place pork chops on a hot grill and cook for 3 to 4 minutes on each side.
5. Serve and enjoy.

Nutrition: Calories: 324, Fat: 26.5 g, Carbs: 2.5 g, Sugar: 1.3 g, Protein: 18 g, Cholesterol: 69 mg

Herb Pork Roast

Preparation Time: 10 minutes
Cooking Time: 14 hours
Servings: 10
Ingredients

- 5 lb pork roast, boneless or bone-in
- 1 tbsp dry herb mix
- 4 garlic cloves, cut into slivers
- 1 tbsp salt

Directions

1. Using a sharp knife make small cuts all over the meat then insert garlic slivers into the cuts.
2. In a small bowl, mix dry herb mix and salt and rub all over the pork roast.
3. Place pork roast in the crock pot.
4. Cover and cook on low for 14 hours.
5. Remove meat from the crock pot and shred using a fork.
6. Serve and enjoy.

Nutrition: Calories: 327, Fat: 8 g, Carbs: 0.5 g, Sugar: 0 g, Protein: 59 g, Cholesterol: 166 mg

Kato Beef Patties

Preparation Time: 10 minutes
Cooking Time: 8 minutes
Servings: 5
Ingredients

- 1 lb ground beef
- 1 egg, lightly beaten
- 3 tbsp almond flour
- 1 small onion, grated
- 2 tbsp fresh parsley, chopped
- 1 tsp dry oregano
- 1 tsp dry mint
- Pepper
- Salt

Directions

1. Add all ingredients into the mixing bowl and mix until combined.
2. Make small patties from the meat mixture.
3. Heat the grill pan over medium-high heat.
4. Place patties in a hot pan and cook for 4 to 5 minutes on each side.
5. Serve and enjoy.

Nutrition: Calories: 188, Fat: 6.6 g, Carbs: 1.7 g, Sugar: 0.7 g, Protein: 28.9 g, Cholesterol: 114 mg

Lemon Beef

Preparation Time: 10 minutes
Cooking Time: 6 hours
Servings: 4
Ingredients

- 1 lb beef chuck roast
- 1 fresh lime juice
- 1 garlic clove, crushed
- 1 tsp chili powder
- 2 cups lemon-lime soda
- ½ tsp salt

Directions

1. Place beef chuck roast into the slow cooker.
2. Season roast with garlic, chili powder, and salt.
3. Pour lemon-lime soda over the roast.
4. Cover the slow cooker with a lid and cook on low for 6 hours. Shred the meat using a fork.
5. Add lime juice over shredded roast and serve.

Nutrition: Calories: 355, Fat: 16.8 g, Carbs: 14 g, Sugar: 11.3 g, Protein: 35.5 g, Cholesterol: 120 mg

Seasoned Pork Chops

Preparation Time: 10 minutes

Cooking Time: 4 hours

Servings: 4

Ingredients

- 4 pork chops
- 2 garlic cloves, minced
- 1 cup chicken broth
- 1 tbsp poultry seasoning
- ¼ cup olive oil
- Pepper and salt

Directions

1. In a bowl, whisk together olive oil, poultry seasoning, garlic, broth, pepper, and salt.
2. Pour the olive oil mixture into the slow cooker then place the pork chops in the crock pot.
3. Cover and cook on high for 4 hours.
4. Serve and enjoy.

Nutrition: Calories: 386, Fat: 32.9 g, Carbs: 3 g, Sugar: 1 g, Protein: 20 g, Cholesterol: 70 mg

Smoky Pork & Cabbage

Preparation Time: 10 minutes

Cooking Time: 8 hours

Servings: 6

Ingredients

- 3 lb pork roast
- ½ cabbage head, chopped
- 1 cup water
- ⅓ cup liquid smoke
- 1 tbsp kosher salt

Directions

1. Rub pork with kosher salt and place into the crock pot.
2. Pour liquid smoke over the pork. Add water.
3. Cover and cook on low for 7 hours.
4. Remove pork from the crock pot and add cabbage to the bottom of the crock pot.
5. Place pork on top of the cabbage.
6. Cover again and cook for 1 hour more.
7. Shred pork with a fork and serve.

Nutrition: Calories: 484, Fat: 21.5 g, Carbs: 4 g, Sugar: 1.9 g, Protein: 66 g, Cholesterol: 195 mg

Tender Lamb Chops

Preparation Time: 10 minutes

Cooking Time: 6 hours

Servings: 8

Ingredients

- 8 lamb chops
- ½ tsp dried thyme
- 1 onion, sliced
- 1 tsp dried oregano
- 2 garlic cloves, minced
- Pepper and salt

Directions

1. Add sliced onion to the slow cooker, as follows:
2. Combine thyme, oregano, salt, and pepper. Rub the chops of lamb.
3. Add garlic to the slow cooker with the lamb chops.
4. Cover the lamb chops with a quarter cup of water.
5. Cook on low for 6 hours with the cover on.
6. Present and savor.

Nutrition: Calories: 40, Fat: 1.9 g, Carbs: 2.3 g, Sugar: 0.6 g, Protein: 3.4 g, Cholesterol: 0 mg

Tomato Pork Chops

Preparation Time: 10 minutes
Cooking Time: 6 hours
Servings: 4
Ingredients

- 4 pork chops, bone-in
- 1 tbsp garlic, minced & ½ small onion, chopped
- 6 oz can tomato paste & 1 bell pepper, chopped
- ¼ tsp red pepper flakes
- 1 tsp Worcestershire sauce
- 1 tbsp dried Italian seasoning
- 14.5 oz can tomatoes, diced
- 2 tsp olive oil
- ¼ tsp pepper
- 1 tsp kosher salt

Directions

1. Heat oil in a pan over medium-high heat.
2. Season pork chops with pepper and salt.
3. Sear pork chops in the pan until brown from both sides.
4. Transfer pork chops into the crock pot.
5. Add remaining ingredients over pork chops.
6. Cover and cook on low for 6 hours.
7. Serve and enjoy.

Nutrition: Calories: 325, Fat: 23.4 g, Carbs: 10 g, Sugar: 6 g, Protein: 20 g, Cholesterol: 70 mg

Pork Cacciatore

Preparation Time: 10 minutes
Cooking Time: 6 hours
Servings: 6
Ingredients
- 1 ½ lb pork chops
- 1 tsp dried oregano
- 1 cup beef broth
- 3 tbsp tomato paste
- 14 oz can tomatoes, diced
- 2 cups mushrooms, sliced
- 1 small onion, diced
- 1 garlic clove, minced
- 2 tbsp olive oil
- ¼ tsp pepper
- ½ tsp salt

Directions
1. In a pan, heat the oil over medium-high heat.
2. Add the pork chops to the pan and cook until both sides are browned.
3. Place the pork chops in the slow cooker.
4. Add the remaining components to the pork chops.
5. Cook on low for 6 hours with the cover on.
6. Present and savor.

Nutrition: Calories: 440, Fat: 33 g, Carbs: 6 g, Sugar: 3 g, Protein: 28 g, Cholesterol: 97 mg

Pork With Tomato & Olives

Preparation Time: 10 minutes

Cooking Time: 30 minutes

Servings: 6

Ingredients

- 6 pork chops, boneless and cut into thick slices
- ⅛ tsp ground cinnamon
- ½ cup olives, pitted and sliced
- 8 oz can tomatoes, crushed
- ¼ cup beef broth
- 2 garlic cloves, chopped
- 1 large onion, sliced
- 1 tbsp olive oil

Directions

1. Heat olive oil in a pan over medium-high heat.
2. Place pork chops in a pan and cook until lightly brown and set aside.
3. Cook garlic and onion in the same pan over medium heat, until onion is softened.
4. Add broth and bring to a boil over high heat.
5. Return pork to pan and stir in crushed tomatoes and remaining ingredients.
6. Cover and simmer for 20 minutes.
7. Serve and enjoy.

Nutrition: Calories: 321, Fat: 23 g, Carbs: 7 g, Sugar: 1 g, Protein: 19g, Cholesterol: 70 mg

Easy Beef Kofta

Preparation Time: 10 minutes
Cooking Time: 10 minutes
Servings: 8
Ingredients
- 2 lb ground beef
- 4 garlic cloves, minced
- 1 onion, minced
- 2 tsp cumin
- 1 cup fresh parsley, chopped
- ¼ tsp pepper
- 1 tsp salt
- Kabab shapes

Directions
1. Add all ingredients into the mixing bowl and mix until combined.
2. Roll the meat mixture into the kabab shapes and cook in a hot pan for 4 to 5 minutes on each side or until cooked.
3. Serve and enjoy.

Nutrition: Calories: 223, Fat: 7.3 g, Carbs: 2.5 g, Sugar: 0.7 g, Protein: 35 g, Cholesterol: 101 mg

Lemon Pepper Pork Tenderloin

Preparation Time: 10 minutes
Cooking Time: 20 minutes
Servings: 4
Ingredients

- 1 lb pork tenderloin
- ¾ tsp lemon pepper
- 2 tsp dried oregano
- 1 tbsp olive oil
- 3 tbsp feta cheese, crumbled
- 3 tbsp olive tapenade

Directions

1. Place the pork, oil, lemon pepper, and oregano in a zip-top bag, rub everything together, and refrigerate for 2 hours.
2. Take the pork out of the zip-lock bag. Make a lengthwise cut across the tenderloin's middle using a sharp knife.
3. Top half of the tenderloin with feta cheese and olive tapenade.
4. Return the second half of the meat to the tenderloin's original shape.
5. Use twine to secure the pork tenderloin at 2-inch intervals.
6. For 20 minutes, grill the pork tenderloin.
7. Slice, and then serve.

Nutrition: Calories: 215, Fat: 9.1 g, Carbs: 1 g, Sugar: 0.5 g, Protein: 30.8 g, Cholesterol: 89 mg

Jalapeno Lamb Patties

Preparation Time: 10 minutes
Cooking Time: 8 minutes
Servings: 4
Ingredients

- 1 lb ground lamb
- 1 jalapeno pepper, minced
- 5 basil leaves, minced
- 10 mint leaves, minced
- ¼ cup fresh parsley, chopped
- 1 cup feta cheese, crumbled
- 1 tbsp garlic, minced
- 1 tsp dried oregano
- ¼ tsp pepper
- ½ tsp kosher salt

Directions

1. Add all ingredients into the mixing bowl and mix until well combined.
2. Preheat the grill to 450°F.
3. Spray the grill with cooking spray.
4. Make 4 equal shape patties from the meat mixture and place them on a hot grill and cook for 3 minutes. Turn the patties to another side and cook for 4 minutes.
5. Serve and enjoy.

Nutrition: Calories: 317, Fat: 16 g, Carbs: 3 g, Sugar: 1.7 g, Protein: 37.5 g, Cholesterol: 135 mg

Basil Parmesan Pork Roast

Preparation Time: 10 minutes

Cooking Time: 6 hours

Servings: 8

Ingredients

- 2 lb lean pork roast, boneless
- 1 tbsp parsley
- ½ cup parmesan cheese, grated
- 28 oz can tomatoes, diced
- 1 tsp dried oregano
- 1 tsp dried basil
- 1 tsp garlic powder
- Pepper
- Salt

Directions

1. Add the meat to the crock pot.
2. Mix tomatoes, oregano, basil, garlic powder, parsley, cheese, pepper, and salt and pour over the meat.
3. Cover and cook on low for 6 hours.
4. Serve and enjoy.

Nutrition: Calories: 294, Fat: 11.6 g, Carbs: 5 g, Sugar: 3 g, Protein: 38 g, Cholesterol: 105 mg

Apricot Pork Meat

Preparation Time: 5 minutes
Cooking Time: 1 hour
Servings: 8
Ingredients

- 3 lb boneless rolled pork
- ½ cup ketchup
- ½ cup teriyaki sauce
- ⅓ cup canned apricots
- ¼ cup cider vinegar
- ¼ cup dark brown sugar, packaged
- 1 tsp paprika
- 1 tsp dried mustard
- ¼ tsp black pepper
- 1 large onion sliced
- 2 cups water

Directions

1. Put the creed meat in a large plastic bag or glass dish. Combine ketchup, teriyaki sauce, canned food, vinegar, brown sugar, paprika, mustard and pepper. Mix together and pour over pork. Refrigerate overnight.
2. Remove the pork from the marinade and keep the marinade. Brown pork on both sides in the pressure cooker over medium heat. Remove pork from the pot.
3. Put the cooking rack, half of the sliced onion and the water inside the pot. Put the pork on the rack of the pot and distribute the remaining onion evenly over the meat. Close and secure the lid.

4. Place the pressure regulator on the vent tube and cook for 60 minutes once the pressure regulator begins to rock slowly.
5. Let the pressure decrease on its own. Put in a saucepan the marinade that it kept and boil until it thickens, stirring occasionally.
6. Remove the meat and onions from the pressure cooker. Add onions to the thickened marinade and serve with sliced pork. Onions can be stepped on before adding to the sauce and served with rice if desired.

Nutrition: Calories: 332, Carbs: 0 g, Fat: 13 g, Protein: 47 g, Sugar: 0 g, Cholesterol: 77 mg

Avocado Peach Salsa on Grilled Swordfish

Preparation Time: 15 minutes
Cooking Time: 10 minutes
Servings: 2
Ingredients

- 1 garlic clove, minced
- 1 lemon juice
- 1 tbsp apple cider vinegar
- 1 tbsp coconut oil
- 1 tsp honey
- swordfish fillets (around 4oz each)
- Pinch cayenne pepper
- A pinch of pepper and salt

Salsa Ingredients:

- ¼ red onion, finely chopped
- ½ cup cilantro, finely chopped
- 1 avocado, halved and diced
- 1 garlic clove, minced
- 2 peaches, seeded and diced
- Juice 1 lime
- Salt to taste

Directions

1. In a shallow dish, mix all swordfish marinade ingredients except the fillet. Mix well then add fillets to marinate. Place in refrigerator for at least an hour.

2. Meanwhile, create salsa by mixing all salsa ingredients in a medium bowl. Put in the refrigerator to cool.
3. Preheat grill and grill fish on medium fire after marinating until cooked around 4 minutes per side.
4. Place each cooked fillet on one serving plate, top with half of the salsa, serve and enjoy.

Nutrition: Calories: 416, Carbs: 21 g, Protein: 30 g, Fat: 23.5 g, Cholesterol: 78 mg

Chapter 9
Vegetable Recipes

VEGETABLE SOUP MOROCCAN STYLE

Preparation Time: 10 minutes
Cooking Time: 1 hour and 15 minutes
Servings: 6
Ingredients

- ½ tsp pepper
- 1 tsp salt & 2 oz whole wheat orzo
- 1 large zucchini, peeled and cut into ¼-inch cubes
- 8 sprigs fresh cilantro, plus more leaves for garnish
- 12 sprigs flat-leaf parsley, plus more for garnish
- A pinch of saffron threads
- 2 stalks celery leaves included, sliced thinly
- 2 carrots, diced
- 2 small turnips, peeled and diced
- 1 14-oz can diced tomatoes
- 6 cups water
- 1 lb lamb stew meat, trimmed and cut into ½-inch cubes
- 2 tsp ground turmeric
- 1 medium onion, diced finely
- 2 tbsp extra virgin olive oil

Directions

1 On medium-high fire, place a large Dutch oven and heat oil.

2. Add turmeric and onion, and stir fry for 2 minutes.
3. Add meat and sauté for 5 minutes.
4. Add saffron, celery, carrots, turnips, tomatoes and juice, and water.
5. With a kitchen string, tie cilantro and parsley sprigs together and into the pot.
6. Cover and bring to a boil. Once boiling, reduce the fire to a simmer and continue to cook for 45 to 50 minutes or until the meat is tender.
7. Once the meat is tender, stir in zucchini. Cover and cook for 8 minutes.
8. Add orzo; cook for 10 minutes or until soft.
9. Remove and discard cilantro and parsley sprigs.
10. Season with pepper and salt.
11. Transfer to a serving bowl and garnish with cilantro and parsley leaves before serving.

Nutrition: Calories: 268, Carbs: 12.9 g, Protein: 28.1 g, Fat: 11.7 g, Cholesterol: 78 mg

Zucchini Garlic Fries

Preparation Time: 15 minutes
Cooking Time: 20 minutes
Servings: 6
Ingredients
- ¼ tsp garlic powder
- ½ cup almond flour
- 2 large egg whites, beaten
- 3 medium zucchinis, sliced into fry sticks
- Salt and pepper to taste

Directions
1. Preheat oven to 400°F.
2. Mix all ingredients in a bowl until the zucchini fries are well coated.
3. Place fries on a cookie sheet and spread evenly.
4. Put in oven and cook for 20 minutes.
5. Halfway through cooking time, stir fries.

Nutrition: Calories: 11, Carbs: 1.1 g, Protein: 1.5 g, Fat: 0.1 g, Cholesterol: 87 mg

Baked Chickpeas

Preparation Time: 15 minutes
Cooking Time: 40 minutes
Servings: 6
Ingredients

- 1 tbsp extra-virgin olive oil
- ½ medium onion, chopped
- 3 garlic cloves, chopped
- 2 tsp smoked paprika
- ¼ tsp ground cumin
- 4 cups halved cherry tomatoes
- 2 (15-ounce) cans chickpeas, drained and rinsed
- ½ cup plain, unsweetened, full-fat Greek yogurt, for serving
- 1 cup crumbled feta, for serving

Directions

1. Preheat the oven to 425°F.
2. In an oven-safe sauté pan or skillet, heat the oil over medium heat and sauté the onion and garlic.
3. Cook for about 5 minutes, until softened and fragrant. Stir in the paprika and cumin and cook for 2 minutes. Stir in the tomatoes and chickpeas.
4. Bring to a simmer for 5 to 10 minutes before placing it in the oven.
5. Roast in the oven for 25 to 30 minutes, until bubbling and thickened. To serve, top with Greek yogurt and feta.

Nutrition: Calories: 330, Carbs: 75.4 g, Protein: 9.0 g, Fat: 18.5 g, Cholesterol: 20 mg

Falafel Bites

Preparation Time: 10 minutes
Cooking Time: 20 minutes
Servings: 4

Ingredients

- 1⅔ cups falafel mix
- 1¼ cups water
- Extra-virgin olive oil spray
- 1 tbsp pickled onions (optional)
- 1 tbsp pickled turnips (optional)
- 2 tbsp Tzatziki sauce (optional)

Directions

1. In a large bowl, carefully stir the falafel mix into the water. Mix well. Let stand for 15 minutes to absorb the water. Form the mix into 1-inch balls and arrange them on a baking sheet.
2. Preheat the broiler to high.
3. Take the balls and flatten them slightly with your thumb (so they won't roll around on the baking sheet). Spray with olive oil, and then broil for 2 to 3 minutes on each side, until crispy and brown.
4. To fry the falafel, fill a pot with ½ inch of cooking oil and heat over medium-high heat to 375°F.
5. Fry the balls for about 3 minutes, until brown and crisp. Drain on paper towels and serve with pickled onions, pickled turnips, and tzatziki sauce (if using).

Nutrition: Calories: 530, Carbs: 95.4 g, Protein: 8.0 g, Fat: 18.5 g, Cholesterol: 11 mg

Quick Vegetable Kebabs

Preparation Time: 15 minutes
Cooking Time: 20 minutes
Servings: 6
Ingredients

- 4 medium red onions, peeled and sliced into 6 wedges
- 4 medium zucchini, cut into 1-inch-thick slices
- 4 bell peppers, cut into 2-inch squares
- 2 yellow bell peppers, cut into 2-inch squares
- 2 orange bell peppers, cut into 2-inch squares
- 2 beefsteak tomatoes, cut into quarters
- 3 tbsp herbed oil

Directions

1. Preheat the oven or grill to medium-high or 350°F.
2. Thread 1 piece of red onion, zucchini, different colored bell peppers, and tomatoes onto a skewer. Repeat until the skewer is full of vegetables, up to 2 inches away from the skewer end, and continue until all skewers are complete.
3. Put the skewers on a baking sheet and cook in the oven for 10 minutes or grill for 5 minutes on each side. The vegetables will be done with they reach your desired crunch or softness.
4. Remove the skewers from the heat and drizzle with herbed oil.

Nutrition: Calories: 235, Carbs: 30.4 g, Protein: 8.0 g, Fat: 14.5 g, Cholesterol: 67 mg

Quinoa With Almonds and Cranberries

Preparation Time: 10 minutes

Cooking Time: 0 minutes

Servings: 4

Ingredients

- 2 cups cooked quinoa
- ⅓ tsp cranberries or currants
- ¼ cup sliced almonds
- 2 garlic cloves, minced
- 1¼ tsp salt
- ½ tsp ground cumin
- ½ tsp turmeric
- ¼ tsp ground cinnamon
- ¼ tsp freshly ground black pepper

Directions

1. In a large bowl, toss the quinoa, cranberries, almonds, garlic, salt, cumin, turmeric, cinnamon, and pepper and stir to combine.
2. Enjoy alone or with roasted cauliflower.

Nutrition: Calories: 430, Carbs: 65.4 g, Protein: 8.0 g, Fat: 15.5 g, Cholesterol: 34 mg

Zucchini Pasta With Mango-Kiwi Sauce

Preparation Time: 5 minutes
Cooking Time: 0 minutes
Servings: 2
Ingredients

- 1 tsp dried herbs – optional
- ½ cup Raw Kale leaves, shredded
- 2 small dried figs
- 3 Medjool dates
- 4 medium kiwis
- 2 big mangoes, seeds discarded
- 2 cup zucchini, spiralized
- ¼ cup roasted cashew

Directions

1. On a salad bowl, place kale then topped with zucchini noodles and sprinkle with dried herbs. Set aside.
2. In a food processor, grind to a powder the cashews. Add figs, dates, kiwis, and mangoes then puree to a smooth consistency.
3. Pour over zucchini pasta, serve and enjoy.

Nutrition: Calories: 530, Carbs: 95.4 g, Protein: 8.0 g, Fat: 18.5 g, Cholesterol: 67 mg

Tortellini in Red Pepper Sauce

Preparation Time: 15 minutes

Cooking Time: 10 minutes

Servings: 4

Ingredients

- 1 (16-ounce) container fresh cheese tortellini (usually green and white pasta)
- 1 (16-ounce) jar roasted red peppers, drained
- 1 tsp garlic powder
- ¼ cup tahini
- 1 tbsp red pepper oil (optional)

Directions

1. Bring a large pot of water to a boil and cook the tortellini according to package directions.
2. In a blender, combine the red peppers with the garlic powder and process until smooth. Once blended, add the tahini until the sauce is thickened. If the sauce gets too thick, add up to 1 tbsp of red pepper oil (if using).
3. Once the tortellini is cooked, drain and leave the pasta in a colander. Add the sauce to the bottom of the empty pot and heat for 2 minutes. Then, add the tortellini back into the pot and cook for 2 more minutes. Serve and enjoy!

Nutrition: Calories: 530, Carbs: 95.4 g, Protein: 8.0 g, Fat: 18.5 g, Cholesterol: 11 mg

Freekeh, Chickpea, and Herb Salad

Preparation Time: 15 minutes

Cooking Time: 0 minutes

Servings: 6

Ingredients

- 1 (15-ounce) can chickpeas, rinsed and drained
- 1 cup cooked freekeh
- 1 cup thinly sliced celery
- 1 bunch scallions, both white and green parts, finely chopped
- ½ cup chopped fresh flat-leaf parsley
- ¼ cup chopped fresh mint
- 3 tbsp chopped celery leaves
- ½ tsp kosher salt
- ⅓ cup extra-virgin olive oil
- ¼ cup freshly squeezed lemon juice
- ¼ tsp cumin seeds
- 1 tsp garlic powder

Directions

1. In a large bowl, combine the chickpeas, freekeh, celery, scallions, parsley, mint, celery leaves, and salt and toss lightly.
2. In a small bowl, whisk together the olive oil, lemon juice, cumin seeds, and garlic powder. Once combined, add to freekeh salad.

Nutrition: Calories: 230, Carbs: 25.4 g, Protein: 8.0 g, Fat: 18.5 g, Cholesterol: 43 mg

Kate's Warm Mediterranean Farro Bowl

Preparation Time: 15 minutes
Cooking Time: 10 minutes
Servings: 4
Ingredients

- ⅓ cup extra-virgin olive oil
- ½ cup chopped red bell pepper
- ⅓ cup chopped red onions
- 2 garlic cloves, minced
- 1 cup zucchini, cut into ½-inch slices
- ½ cup canned chickpeas, drained and rinsed
- ½ cup coarsely chopped artichokes
- 3 cups cooked farro
- Salt
- Freshly ground black pepper
- ¼ cup sliced olives, for serving (optional)
- ½ cup crumbled feta cheese, for serving (optional)
- 2 tbsp fresh basil, chiffonade, for serving (optional)
- 3 tbsp balsamic reduction, for serving (optional)

Directions

1. In a large sauté pan or skillet, heat the oil over medium heat and sauté the pepper, onions, and garlic for about 5 minutes, until tender.
2. Add the zucchini, chickpeas, and artichokes, then stir and continue to sauté vegetables, approximately 5 more minutes, until just soft.
3. Stir in the cooked farro, tossing to combine and cooking

enough to heat through. Season with salt and pepper and remove from the heat.

4. Transfer the contents of the pan to the serving vessels or bowls.

5. Top with olives, feta, and basil (if using). Drizzle with balsamic reduction (if using) to finish.

Nutrition: Calories: 530, Carbs: 95.4 g, Protein: 8.0 g, Fat: 13.5 g, Cholesterol: 63 mg

Creamy Chickpea Sauce With Whole-Wheat Fusilli

Preparation Time: 15 minutes
Cooking Time: 20 minutes
Servings: 4

Ingredients

- ¼ cup extra-virgin olive oil
- ½ large shallot, chopped
- 5 garlic cloves, thinly sliced
- 1 (15-ounce) can chickpeas, drained and rinsed, reserving ½ cup canning liquid
- 1 cup whole-grain fusilli pasta

Directions

1. Sauté the shallot and garlic in a medium pan with the oil over medium heat for 3 to 5 minutes, or until the garlic is brown. 2 tbsp of the can's liquid and
2. ¾ of the chickpeas are added, and the mixture is simmered.
3. Take the mixture from the heat, put it in a regular blender, and puree until smooth. Add the leftover chickpeas at this point. If it gets too thick, add more of the reserved chickpea juice.
4. Bring a large pot of salted water to a boil, then cook the pasta for about 8 minutes, or until it is al dente. After draining the pasta, add it back to the pot with 12 cups of the reserved pasta water.
5. Add up to ¼ cup of the chickpea sauce to the hot pasta.

Nutrition: Calories: 230, Carbs: 20.4 g, Protein: 8.0 g, Fat: 18.5 g, Cholesterol: 76 mg

Tomato Basil Cauliflower Rice

Preparation Time: 5 minutes

Cooking Time: 10 minutes

Servings: 4

Ingredients

- Salt and pepper to taste
- Dried parsley for garnish
- ¼ cup tomato paste
- ½ tsp garlic, minced
- ½ tsp onion powder
- ½ tsp marjoram
- 1 ½ tsp dried basil
- 1 tsp dried oregano
- 1 large head cauliflower
- 1 tsp oil

Directions

1. Cut the cauliflower into florets and place it in the food processor.
2. Pulse until it has a coarse consistency similar to rice. Set aside.
3. In a skillet, heat the oil and sauté the garlic and onion for 3 minutes. Add the rest of the ingredients. Cook for 8 minutes.

Nutrition: Calories: 106, Carbs: 15.1 g, Protein: 3.3 g, Fat: 5.0 g, Cholesterol: 66 mg

Vegan Sesame Tofu and Eggplants

Preparation Time: 10 minutes
Cooking Time: 20 minutes
Servings: 4
Ingredients

- 5 tbsp olive oil
- 1 lb firm tofu, sliced
- 3 tbsp rice vinegar
- 2 tsp Swerve sweetener
- 2 whole eggplants, sliced
- ¼ cup soy sauce
- Salt and pepper to taste
- 4 tbsp toasted sesame oil
- ¼ cup sesame seeds
- 1 cup fresh cilantro, chopped

Directions

1. Heat the oil in a pan for 2 minutes.
2. Fry the tofu for 3 minutes on each side.
3. Stir in the rice vinegar, sweetener, eggplants, and soy sauce. Season with salt and pepper to taste.
4. Cover and cook for 5 minutes on medium fire. Stir and continue cooking for another 5 minutes.
5. Toss in the sesame oil, sesame seeds, and cilantro.
6. Serve and enjoy.

Nutrition: Calories: 616, Carbs: 27.4 g, Protein: 23.9 g, Fat: 49.2 g, Cholesterol: 55 mg

Vegetarian Coconut Curry

Preparation Time: 10 minutes
Cooking Time: 10 minutes
Servings: 4
Ingredients

- 4 tbsp coconut oil
- 1 medium onion, chopped
- 1 tsp minced garlic
- 1 tsp minced ginger
- 1 cup broccoli florets
- 2 cups fresh spinach leaves
- 2 tsp fish sauce
- 1 tbsp garam masala
- ½ cup coconut milk
- Salt and pepper to taste

Directions

1. Heat oil in a pot.
2. Sauté the onion and garlic until fragrant, around 3 minutes.
3. Stir in the rest of the ingredients, except for spinach leaves.
4. Season with salt and pepper to taste.
5. Cover and cook on medium fire for 5 minutes.
6. Stir and add spinach leaves. Cover and cook for another 2 minutes.
7. Turn off the fire and let it sit for 2 more minutes before serving.

Nutrition: Calories: 210, Carbs: 6.5 g, Protein: 2.1 g, Fat: 20.9 g, Cholesterol: 65 mg

Chapter 10
Soups Recipes

Spring Farro Plate

Preparation Time: 15 minutes
Cooking Time: 0 minutes
Servings: 6
Ingredients

- 1 cup farro, cooked
- 2 cups baby spinach
- 2 grapefruits, roughly chopped
- 2 tbsp balsamic vinegar
- ¼ tsp white pepper
- 1 tbsp olive oil

Directions

1. Mix baby spinach and farro in the big bowl.
2. Then add grapefruit and shake the ingredients well.
3. Transfer the mixture to the serving plates and sprinkle with white pepper, olive oil, and balsamic vinegar.

Nutrition: Calories: 113, Protein: 12.3 g, Carbs: 33.4 g, Fat: 19.3 g, Cholesterol: 23 mg

Sorghum Tabbouleh

Preparation Time: 10 minutes
Cooking Time: 0 minutes
Servings: 2
Ingredients

- 2 oz sorghum, cooked
- 3 oz pumpkin, diced, boiled
- ½ white onion, diced
- 1 date, pitted, chopped
- 1 tbsp avocado oil
- ½ tsp liquid honey
- 2 oz Feta, crumbled

Directions

1. Put sorghum, pumpkin, onion, and date in the big bowl.
2. Then sprinkle the ingredients with avocado oil and liquid honey. Stir well.
3. Transfer the cooked tabbouleh to the serving plates and top with crumbled feta.

Nutrition: Calories: 123, Protein: 12.3 g, Carbs: 33.4 g, Fat: 19.3 g, Cholesterol: 78 mg

Roasted Sorghum

Preparation Time: 10 minutes
Cooking Time: 15 minutes
Servings: 4
Ingredients
- 1 tbsp avocado oil
- ½ cup sorghum, cooked
- 1 carrot, diced
- 2 tbsp dried parsley
- ½ tsp dried oregano
- 2 tbsp cream cheese

Directions
1. Heat avocado oil and add the carrot.
2. Roast it for 5 minutes.
3. Then add cooked sorghum, parsley, oregano, and cream cheese.
4. Roast the meal for 10 minutes on low heat. Stir it from time to time to avoid burning.

Nutrition: Calories: 123, Protein: 2.3 g, Carbs: 3.4 g, Fat: 9.3 g, Cholesterol: 56 mg

Sorghum Stew

Preparation Time: 10 minutes
Cooking Time: 25 minutes
Servings: 5
Ingredients

- 1 cup sorghum
- ½ cup ground sausages
- ½ cup tomatoes
- 1 jalapeno pepper, chopped
- ½ cup bell pepper, chopped
- 4 cups chicken stock

Directions

1. Roast the sausages for 5 minutes in the saucepan.
2. Then add tomatoes, jalapeno, and bell pepper.
3. Cook the ingredients for 10 minutes.
4. After this, add sorghum and chicken stock and boil the stew for 10 minutes more.

Nutrition: Calories: 127, Protein: 12.3 g, Carbs: 13.4 g, Fat: 19.3 g, Cholesterol: 43 mg

Roasted Red Pepper and Tomato Soup

Preparation Time: 10 minutes
Cooking Time: 55 minutes
Servings: 4

Ingredients

- 2 red bell peppers, seeded and halved
- 3 tomatoes, cored and halved
- ½ medium onion, quartered
- 2 cloves garlic, peeled and halved
- 1 to 2 tbsp olive oil
- ¼ tsp salt
- ¼ tsp ground black pepper
- 2 cups vegetable broth
- 2 tbsp tomato paste
- ¼ cup fresh parsley, chopped
- ¼ tsp Italian seasoning blend
- ¼ tsp ground paprika
- ⅛ tsp ground cayenne pepper, or more to taste

Directions

1. Preheat your oven to 375°F.
2. Grab a medium bowl and add the red peppers, tomatoes, onion, garlic, olive oil, and salt and pepper. Toss well to coat.
3. Place onto a baking sheet and pop into the oven for 45 minutes until soft.
4. Next, place the veggie broth over medium heat and add the roasted veggies, tomato paste, parsley, paprika, and cayenne.

5. Stir to combine then simmer for 10 minutes.
6. Use an immersion blender to puree the soup then return back to the pan.
7. Reheat if required, add extra seasoning then serve and enjoy.

Nutrition: Calories: 531, Protein: 26.3 g, Carbs: 33.4 g, Fat: 30.3 g, Cholesterol: 76 mg

Fast Seafood Gumbo

Preparation Time: 10 minutes
Cooking Time: 40 minutes
Servings: 4
Ingredients
- ¼ cup olive oil
- ¼ cup flour
- 1 medium white onion, chopped
- 1 cup celery, chopped
- 1 red or green bell pepper, chopped and deseeded
- 1 red chili, chopped
- 2 cups okra, chopped
- 1 cup canned crushed tomatoes
- 2 large cloves garlic, crushed
- 1 tsp dried thyme
- 2 cups fish stock
- 1 bay leaf
- 1 tsp cayenne powder
- 2x8 oz. Can crab meat with brine
- 1 lb Shrimp, peeled and deveined
- Salt & pepper, to taste

Directions
1. Find a large pan, add the oil and place over medium heat.
2. Add the flour and stir well until it forms a thick paste.
3. Add the onions, celery, peppers, and okra and stir well, cooking for 5 minutes.

4. Add the garlic, tomatoes, thyme, stock, bay leaf, and cayenne and stir again.
5. Bring to a boil, then reduce the heat and simmer for 15 minutes.
6. Add the shrimp and crab and cook for 8 minutes more.

Nutrition: Calories: 551, Protein: 36.3 g, Carbs: 33.4 g, Fat: 30.3 g, Cholesterol: 76 mg

Greek Spring Soup

Preparation Time: 10 minutes
Cooking Time: 35 minutes
Servings: 4

Ingredients

- 6 cups chicken broth
- 1 ½ cups diced or shredded cooked chicken
- 2 tbsp olive oil
- 1 small onion, diced
- 1 bay leaf
- ⅓ cup arborio rice
- 1 large free-range egg
- 2 tbsp water
- Juice ½ lemon
- 1 cup chopped asparagus
- 1 cup diced carrots
- ½ cup fresh chopped dill, divided
- Salt and pepper, to taste

Directions

1. Find a large pan, add the oil and place over medium heat.
2. Add the onions and cook for 5 minutes until soft.
3. Next add ¼ cup dill, plus the chicken broth and bay leaf. Bring to a boil.
4. Add the rice and reduce the heat to low. Simmer for 10 minutes.
5. Add the carrots and asparagus and cook for 10 more minutes

until the rice and veggies are tender.

6. Add the chicken and simmer.
7. Meanwhile, find a medium bowl and add the egg, lemon, and water. Whisk well.
8. Add ½ cup of the stock to the egg mixture, stirring constantly then pour it all back into the pot.
9. Heat through and allow the soup to thicken.
10. Add remaining dill, season well with salt and pepper, then serve and enjoy.

Nutrition: Calories: 551, Protein: 16.3 g, Carbs: 23.4 g, Fat: 10.3 g, Cholesterol: 78 mg

Lemon Chicken Soup

Preparation Time: 10 minutes
Cooking Time: 20 minutes
Servings: 6

Ingredients

- 10 cups chicken broth
- 3 tbsp olive oil
- 8 cloves garlic, minced
- 1 sweet onion, sliced
- 1 large lemon, zested
- 2 boneless skinless chicken breasts
- ½ tsp crushed red pepper
- 2 oz. crumbled feta
- ⅓ cup chopped chive
- Salt and pepper, to taste

Directions

1. Grab a stock pot, add the oil and place over medium heat.
2. Add the onion and garlic and cook for 5 minutes until soft.
3. Add the broth, chicken breasts, lemon zest, and crushed pepper.
4. Raise the heat, cover and bring to a boil.
5. Reduce the heat then simmer for 5 minutes.
6. Turn off the heat, remove the lid and remove the chicken from the pot.
7. Pop onto a place and use 2 forks to shred.
8. Pop back into the pot, add the feta, chives and salt and pepper.

9   Stir well then serve and enjoy.

Nutrition: Calories: 251, Protein: 16.3 g, Carbs: 23.4 g, Fat: 30.3 g, Cholesterol: 53 mg

Tuscan Vegetable Pasta Soup

Preparation Time: 10 minutes
Cooking Time: 20 minutes
Servings: 6
Ingredients

- 2 tbsp extra virgin olive oil
- 4 cloves garlic, minced
- 1 medium yellow onion, diced
- ½ cup carrot, chopped
- ½ cup celery, chopped
- 1 medium zucchini, sliced and quartered
- 1 x 15 oz. Can diced tomatoes
- 6 cups vegetable stock
- 2 tbsp tomato paste
- 6 to 8 oz. whole wheat pasta
- 1 x 15 oz. Can white beans
- 2 large handfuls baby spinach
- 6 basil cubes
- Salt and pepper, to taste

Directions

1. Grab a stock pot, add the oil and pop over medium heat.
2. Add the onion and garlic and cook for 5 minutes until soft.
3. Throw in the carrots, celery, and zucchini and cook for an extra 5 minutes, stirring occasionally.
4. Add the tomato and salt and pepper and cook for 1 to 2 minutes.

5. Add the veggies broth and tomato paste, stir well then bring to a boil.
6. Throw in the pasta, cook for 10 minutes then add the spinach, white beans, basil cubes and seasoning.
7. Stir well then remove from the heat.
8. Divide between large bowls and serve and enjoy.

Nutrition: Calories: 151, Protein: 26.3 g, Carbs: 14.4 g, Fat: 30.3 g, Cholesterol: 67 mg

Dairy-Free Zucchini Soup

Preparation Time: 10 minutes
Cooking Time: 20 minutes
Servings: 8
Ingredients

- 2½ lb Zucchini
- 1 medium onion, diced
- 2 tbsp olive oil
- 4 garlic cloves, chopped
- 4 cups chicken stock
- Sea salt and pepper, to taste
- ⅓ cup fresh basil leaves

Directions

1. Grab a pan, add the oil and pop over medium heat.
2. Add the onion, garlic, and zucchini and cook for 5 minutes until soft.
3. Add the stock and simmer for 15 minutes.
4. Remove from the heat, stir through the basil, add the seasoning and use an immersion blender to whizz until smooth.
5. Serve and enjoy.

Nutrition: Calories: 551, Protein: 36.3 g, Carbs: 33.4 g, Fat: 30.3 g, Cholesterol: 87 mg

Farro Stew With Kale & Cannellini Beans

Preparation Time: 10 minutes
Cooking Time: 40 minutes
Servings: 4
Ingredients

- 2 tbsp olive oil
- 2 medium carrots, diced
- 1 medium onion, chopped
- 2 sticks celery, chopped
- 2 cloves garlic, minced
- 3 cups low-sodium vegetable broth
- 1 x 14.5 oz. Can diced tomatoes
- 1 cup farro, rinsed
- 1 tsp dried oregano
- 1 bay leaf
- Salt, to taste
- ½ cup parsley
- 2 cups chopped kale, thick ribs removed
- 1 x 15 oz. Can cannellini beans, drained and rinsed
- 1 tbsp fresh lemon juice

Directions

1. Grab a stock pot, add the oil and place over medium heat.
2. Add the onion, carrots, and celery and cook for 5 minutes until becoming soft.
3. Add the garlic and cook for another 30 seconds.
4. Stir through the broth, tomatoes, farro, oregano, bay leaf,

parsley, and salt.

5   Cover with the lid and bring to a boil. Reduce the heat then simmer for 20 minutes.

6   Remove the lid, add the kale and cook for a further 10 to 15 minutes.

7   Remove the bay leaf, add the beans, stir through the lemon juice and any additional liquid then stir well to combine.

8   Serve and enjoy.

Nutrition: Calories: 21, Protein: 16.3 g, Carbs: 3.4 g, Fat: 6.3 g, Cholesterol: 98 mg

Greek Style Spring Soup

Preparation Time: 10 minutes

Cooking Time: 20 minutes

Servings: 4

Ingredients

- 3 cups chicken stock
- ½ lb chicken breast, shredded
- 1 tbsp chives, chopped
- 1 egg, whisked
- ½ white onion, diced
- 1 bell pepper, chopped
- 1 tbsp olive oil
- ¼ cup arborio rice
- ½ tsp salt
- 1 tbsp fresh cilantro, chopped

Directions

1. Pour olive oil into the stock pan and preheat it.
2. Add onion and bell pepper. Roast the vegetables for 3 to 4 minutes. Stir them from time to time.
3. After this, add rice and stir well.
4. Cook the ingredients for 3 minutes over medium heat.
5. Then add chicken stock and stir the soup well.
6. Add salt and bring the soup to a boil.
7. Add shredded chicken breast, cilantro, and chives. Add egg and stir it carefully.
8. Close the lid and simmer the soup for 5 minutes over medium heat.
9. Remove the cooked soup from the heat.

Nutrition: Calories: 176, Fat: 5.6 g, Fiber: 7.6 g, Carbs: 23.6 g, Protein: 4.6 g, Cholesterol: 98 mg

Chapter 11
Snack and Appetizers Recipes

159. Pistachio Arugula Salad

Preparation Time: 10 minutes

Cooking Time: 0 minutes

Servings: 6

Ingredients
- 5 Cups Kale, Chopped
- ¼ Cup Olive Oil
- 2 tbsp Lemon Juice, Fresh
- ½ tsp Smoked Paprika
- 2 Cups Arugula
- ⅓ Cup Pistachios, Unsalted & Shelled

Directions
1. Get out a salad bowl and combine your oil, lemon, smoked paprika, and kale. Gently massage the leaves for ½ minute. Your kale should be coated well.
2. Gently mix your arugula and pistachios when ready to serve.

Nutrition: Calories: 150, Protein: 5 g, Fat: 12 g, Carbs: 8 g, Cholesterol: 123 mg

Asparagus Couscous

Preparation Time: 15 minutes
Cooking Time: 30 minutes
Servings: 6
Ingredients

- 1 cup goat cheese, garlic & herb flavored
- 1 ½ lb asparagus, trimmed & chopped into 1-inch pieces
- 1 tbsp olive oil
- 1 clove garlic, minced
- ¼ tsp black pepper
- 1 ¾ cup water
- 8 ounces whole wheat couscous, uncooked
- ¼ tsp sea salt, fine

Directions

1. Start by heating your oven to 425°F, and then put your goat cheese on the counter. It needs to come to room temperature.
2. Get out a bowl and mix your oil, pepper, garlic, and asparagus. Spread the asparagus on a baking sheet and roast for 10 minutes. Make sure to stir at least once.
3. Remove it from the pan, and place your asparagus in a serving bowl.
4. Get out a medium saucepan, and bring your water to a boil. Add in your salt and couscous. Reduce the heat to medium-low, and then cover your saucepan. Cook for 20 minutes. All your water should be absorbed.
5. Pour the couscous into a bowl with asparagus, and ad din your goat cheese. Stir until melted, and serve warm.

Nutrition: Calories: 263, Protein: 11 g, Fat: 9 g, Carbs: 36 g, Cholesterol: 134 mg

Easy Salad Wraps

Preparation Time: 10 minutes
Cooking Time: 0 minutes
Servings: 4

Ingredients

- 1 ½ cups cucumber, seedless, peeled & chopped
- 1 cup tomato, chopped
- ½ cup mint, fresh & chopped fine
- 1 oz can black olives, sliced & drained
- ¼ cup red onion, diced
- 2 tbsp olive oil
- Sea salt & black pepper to taste
- 1 tbsp red wine vinegar
- ½ cup goat cheese, crumbled
- 4 flatbread wraps, whole wheat

Directions

1. Get out a bowl and mix your tomato, mint, cucumber, onion, and olives.
2. Get out another bowl and whisk your vinegar, oil, pepper, and salt. Drizzle this over your salad, and mix well.
3. Spread your goat cheese over the 4 wraps, and then spoon your salad filling in each one. Fold up to serve.

Nutrition: Calories: 262, Protein: 7 g, Fat: 15 g, Carbs: 23 g, Cholesterol: 78 mg

Vegetable Panini

Preparation Time: 15 minutes
Cooking Time: 25 Minutes
Servings: 4
Ingredients

- 2 tbsp olive oil, divided
- ¼ cup onion, diced
- 1 cup zucchini, diced
- 1 ½ cups broccoli, diced
- ¼ tsp oregano
- Sea salt & black pepper to taste
- 12 oz jar roasted red peppers, drained & chopped fine
- 2 tbsp Parmesan cheese, grated
- 1 cup mozzarella, fresh & sliced
- 2 foot-long whole grain Italian loaf, cut into 4 pieces

Directions

1. Heat your oven to 450°F, and then get out a baking sheet. Heat the oven with your baking sheet inside.
2. Get out a bowl and mix your broccoli, zucchini, oregano, pepper, onion, and salt with a tbsp of olive oil.
3. Remove your baking sheet from the oven and coat it with nonstick cooking spray. Spread the vegetable mixture over it to roast for 5 minutes. Stir halfway through.
4. Remove it from the oven, add your red pepper, and sprinkle with Parmesan cheese. Mix everything together.
5. Get out a panini maker or grill pan, and place it over medium-high heat.
6. Heat up a tbsp of oil.

7. Spread the bread horizontally on it, but don't cut it all the way through. Fill with the vegetable mix, and then a slice of mozzarella cheese on top. Close the sandwich and cook like you would a normal panini. With a press, it should grill for 5 minutes. For a grill pan cook for 2 minutes per side. Repeat for the remaining sandwiches.

Nutrition: Calories: 352, Protein: 16 g, Fat: 15 g, Carbs: 45 g, Cholesterol: 67 mg

Baked Tomato

Preparation Time: 7 minutes

Cooking Time: 25 Minutes

Servings: 4

Ingredients

- Whole grain bread
- Salt and pepper to taste
- 1 tbsp finely chopped basil
- 2 cloves garlic. Finely chopped
- Extra virgin oil
- 2 large tomatoes

Directions

1. Preheat your oven to 400°F.
2. Use the olive oil to brush the bottom of a baking dish. Set aside.
3. Slice the tomatoes into a thickness of ½ inch. Lay the tomato pieces into the baking dish that you had prepared earlier. Sprinkle some basil and garlic on top of the tomatoes, and season with pepper and salt to taste.
4. Then drizzle the slices of tomatoes with olive oil and then place the baking dish into the oven. Bake for about 20 to 25 minutes.
5. Remove from the oven, give it a few seconds to cool down and then serve and enjoy.
6. The tomato juice and olive oil at the bottom of the pan can be used as a dipping sauce. So if you want, you can put it into a small bowl and enjoy it with warm whole-grain bread.

Nutrition: Calories: 342, Protein: 16 g, Fat: 10 g, Carbs: 45 g, Cholesterol: 67 mg

Humus Filled Roasted Veggies

Preparation Time: 7 minutes
Cooking Time: 15 Minutes
Servings: 12
Ingredients

- 6 pitted kalamata olives quartered
- ½ cup (2 oz) feta cheese
- 1 cup hummus
- 2 tbsp olive oil
- 1 medium red bell pepper
- 1 small zucchini (6-inch)

Directions

1. Heat a closed medium-sized contact grill at 375°F for about 5 minutes.
2. Cut the zucchini into half lengthwise. Use a spoon to scoop out the seeds from the 2 vegetables and discard the seeds. Cut the red bell pepper around the stem and remove the stem and the seeds; cut them into quarters and set aside.
3. Use olive oil to brush the bell pepper, and zucchini pieces. Once done, place them on the grill. Do not close the grill. Cook them for 4 to 6 minutes and turn them only once. The vegetables should be tender by the end of the 6th minute. Remove from the grill and let them cool for 2 minutes. Cut the vegetables into 1-inch pieces.
4. Use a spoon to scoop 2 tbsp of humus onto each piece of vegetable. Light drizzle the vegetables with cheese and top it with 1 piece of olive. Serve cold or warm.

Nutrition: Calories: 342, Protein: 10 g, Fat: 1 g, Carbs: 35 g, Cholesterol: 45 mg

Healthy Coconut Blueberry Balls

Preparation Time: 10 minutes
Cooking Time: 1 minute
Servings: 12

Ingredients

- ¼ cup flaked coconut
- ¼ cup blueberries
- ½ tsp vanilla
- ¼ cup honey
- ½ cup creamy almond butter
- ¼ tsp cinnamon
- 1 ½ tbsp chia seeds
- ¼ cup flaxseed meal
- 1 cup rolled oats, gluten-free

Directions

1. In a large bowl, add oats, cinnamon, chia seeds, and a flaxseed meal and mix well.
2. Add almond butter to a microwave-safe bowl and microwave for 30 seconds. Stir until smooth.
3. Add vanilla and honey in melted almond butter and stir well.
4. Pour the almond butter mixture over the oat mixture and stir to combine.
5. Add coconut and blueberries and stir well.
6. Make small balls from the oat mixture and place them onto the baking tray and place them in the refrigerator for 1 hour.
7. Serve and enjoy.

Nutrition: Calories: 129, Fat: 7.4 g, Carbs: 14.1 g, Sugar: 7 g, Protein: 4 g, Cholesterol: 0 mg

Crunchy Roasted Chickpeas

Preparation Time: 10 minutes

Cooking Time: 25 minutes

Servings: 4

Ingredients

- 15 oz can chickpeas, drained, rinsed and pat dry
- ¼ tsp paprika
- 1 tbsp olive oil
- ¼ tsp pepper
- A pinch of salt

Directions

1. Preheat the oven to 450°F.
2. Spray a baking tray with cooking spray and set aside.
3. In a large bowl, toss chickpeas with olive oil and spread chickpeas onto the prepared baking tray.
4. Roast chickpeas in preheated oven for 25 minutes. Shake after every 10 minutes.
5. Once the chickpeas are done then immediately toss them with paprika, pepper, and salt.
6. Serve and enjoy.

Nutrition: Calories: 157, Fat: 4.7 g, Carbs: 24.2 g, Sugar: 0 g, Protein: 5.3 g, Cholesterol: 0 mg

Tasty Zucchini Chips

Preparation Time: 10 minutes
Cooking Time: 15 minutes
Servings: 8
Ingredients

- 2 medium zucchini, sliced 4mm thick
- ½ tsp paprika
- ¼ tsp garlic powder
- ¾ cup parmesan cheese, grated
- 4 tbsp olive oil
- ¼ tsp pepper
- Pinch of salt

Directions

1. Preheat the oven to 375°F.
2. Spray a baking tray with cooking spray and set aside.
3. In a bowl, combine the oil, garlic powder, paprika, pepper, and salt.
4. Add sliced zucchini and toss to coat.
5. Arrange zucchini slices onto the prepared baking tray and sprinkle grated cheese on top.
6. Bake in preheated oven for 15 minutes or until lightly golden brown.
7. Serve and enjoy.

Nutrition: Calories: 110, Fat: 9.8 g, Carbs: 2.2 g, Sugar: 0.9 g, Protein: 4.4 g, Cholesterol: 7 mg

Roasted Green Beans

Preparation Time: 10 minutes
Cooking Time: 15 minutes
Servings: 4
Ingredients

- 1 lb green beans
- 4 tbsp parmesan cheese
- 2 tbsp olive oil
- ¼ tsp garlic powder
- Pinch of salt

Directions

1. Preheat the oven to 400°F.
2. Add green beans to a large bowl.
3. Add remaining ingredients on top of green beans and toss to coat.
4. Spread green beans onto the baking tray and roast in preheated oven for 15 minutes. Stir halfway through.
5. Serve and enjoy.

Nutrition: Calories: 101, Fat: 7.5 g, Carbs: 8.3 g, Sugar: 1.6 g, Protein: 2.6 g, Cholesterol: 1 mg

Savory Pistachio Balls

Preparation Time: 10 minutes
Cooking Time: 0 minutes
Servings: 16
Ingredients

- ½ cup pistachios, unsalted
- 1 cup dates, pitted
- ½ tsp ground fennel seeds
- ½ cup raisins
- Pinch of pepper

Directions

1. Add all ingredients into the food processor and process until well combined.
2. Make small balls and place them onto the baking tray and place them in the refrigerator for 1 hour.
3. Serve and enjoy.

Nutrition: Calories: 55, Fat: 0.9 g, Carbs: 12.5 g, Sugar: 9.9 g, Protein: 0.8 g, Cholesterol: 0 mg

Roasted Almonds

Preparation Time: 10 minutes
Cooking Time: 20 minutes
Servings: 12
Ingredients
- 2½ cups almonds
- ¼ tsp cayenne
- ¼ tsp ground coriander
- ¼ tsp cumin
- ¼ tsp chili powder
- 1 tbsp fresh rosemary, chopped
- 1 tbsp olive oil
- 2 ½ tbsp maple syrup
- Pinch of salt

Directions
1. Preheat the oven to 325°F.
2. Spray a baking tray with cooking spray and set aside.
3. In a mixing bowl, whisk together oil, cayenne, coriander, cumin, chili powder, rosemary, maple syrup, and salt.
4. Add almonds and stir to coat.
5. Spread almonds onto the prepared baking tray.
6. Roast almonds in preheated oven for 20 minutes. Stir halfway through.
7. Serve and enjoy.

Nutrition: Calories: 137, Fat: 11.2 g, Carbs: 7.3 g, Sugar: 3.3 g, Protein: 4.2 g, Cholesterol: 0 mg

Banana Strawberry Popsicles

Preparation Time: 5 minutes

Cooking Time: 0 minutes

Servings: 8

Ingredients

- ½ cup Greek yogurt
- 1 banana, peeled and sliced
- 1 ¼ cups fresh strawberries
- ¼ cup water

Directions

1. Add all ingredients into the blender and blend until smooth.
2. Pour the blended mixture into the popsicle molds and place in the refrigerator for 4 hours or until set.
3. Serve and enjoy.

Nutrition: Calories: 31, Fat: 0 g, Carbs: 6.2 g, Sugar: 4 g, Protein: 1.2 g, Cholesterol: 1 mg

Chocolate Matcha Balls

Preparation Time: 10 minutes
Cooking Time: 5 minutes
Servings: 15

Ingredients

- 2 tbsp unsweetened cocoa powder
- 3 tbsp oats, gluten-free
- ½ cup pine nuts
- ½ cup almonds
- 1 cup dates, pitted
- 2 tbsp matcha powder

Directions

1. Add oats, pine nuts, almonds, cocoa powder, and dates into a food processor and process until well combined.
2. Place matcha powder in a small dish.
3. Make small balls from the mixture and coat them with matcha powder.
4. Enjoy or store in the refrigerator until ready to eat.

Nutrition: Calories: 88, Fat: 4.9 g, Carbs: 11.3 g, Sugar: 7.8 g, Protein: 1.9 g, Cholesterol: 0 mg

Chia Almond Butter Pudding

Preparation Time: 5 minutes
Cooking Time: 0 minutes
Servings: 1
Ingredients

- ¼ cup chia seeds
- 1 cup unsweetened almond milk
- 1 ½ tbsp maple syrup
- 2 ½ tbsp almond butter

Directions

1. Add almond milk, maple syrup, and almond butter in a bowl and stir well.
2. Add chia seeds and stir to mix.
3. Pour the pudding mixture into the Mason jar and place it in the refrigerator overnight.
4. Serve and enjoy.

Nutrition: Calories: 354, Fat: 21.3 g, Carbs: 31.1 g, Sugar: 18.9 g, Protein: 11.2 g, Cholesterol: 0 mg

Refreshing Strawberry Popsicles

Preparation Time: 5 minutes

Cooking Time: 0 minutes

Servings: 8

Ingredients

- ½ cup almond milk
- 2½ cups fresh strawberries

Directions

1. Add strawberries and almond milk into the blender and blend until smooth.
2. Pour strawberry mixture into popsicle molds and place in the refrigerator for 4 hours or until set.
3. Serve and enjoy.

Nutrition: Calories: 49, Fat: 3.7 g, Carbs: 4.3 g, Sugar: 2.7 g, Protein: 0.6 g, Cholesterol: 0 mg

Dark Chocolate Mousse

Preparation Time: 10 minutes

Cooking Time: 10 minutes

Servings: 4

Ingredients

- 3 oz unsweetened dark chocolate, grated
- ½ tsp vanilla
- 1 tbsp honey
- 2 cups Greek yogurt
- ¾ cup unsweetened almond milk

Directions

1. Add chocolate and almond milk to a saucepan and heat over medium heat until just the chocolate melted. Do not boil.
2. Once the chocolate and almond milk are combined then add vanilla and honey and stir well.
3. Add yogurt to a large mixing bowl.
4. Pour the chocolate mixture on top of the yogurt and mix until well combined.
5. Pour the chocolate yogurt mixture into the serving bowls and place in the refrigerator for 2 hours.
6. Top with fresh raspberries and serve.

Nutrition: Calories: 278, Fat: 15.4 g, Carbs: 20 g, Sugar: 13 g, Protein: 10.5 g, Cholesterol: 7 mg

Cucumber and Nuts Salad

Preparation Time: 20 minutes
Cooking Time: 0 minutes
Servings: 10

Ingredients

- 1 ½ cup (2 oz) crumbled feta cheese
- ⅓ cup chopped walnuts, toasted
- 1 chopped orange, peeled and sectioned
- ½ tsp salt
- 1 tbsp grated orange peel
- ⅓ cup chopped fresh mint leaves that are loosely packed
- ⅓ cup loosely packed flat-leafed chopped parsley
- ½ cup sweetened dried cranberries
- ½ cup chopped red onion
- ½ medium cucumber, unpeeled, seeded and chopped
- 2 tbsp olive oil
- ¼ cup orange juice
- 1 cup boiling water
- 1 cup uncooked bulgur

Directions

1. Start by placing the bulgur in a large heatproof bowl. Pour some hot boiling water into the heatproof bowl and stir the mixture. Let the bulgur sit for about 1 hour or until the water has been absorbed.
2. Add in orange peel, mint, parsley, cranberries, onion, cucumber, salt, oil, and orange juice and toss well. Cover the large bowl and refrigerate it for 2 to 3 hours or until the

mixture is chilled.

3. Remove the mixture from the fridge and stir in some chopped oranges. Lightly sprinkle the mixture with cheese and walnuts. Serve and enjoy.

Nutrition: Calories: 252, Protein: 16 g, Fat: 10 g, Carbs: 35 g, Cholesterol: 8 mg

Tuna Salad

Preparation Time: 10 minutes
Cooking Time: 0 minutes
Servings: 4
Ingredients

- 10 cherry tomatoes, quartered
- 4 scallions, trimmed and sliced
- 2 tbsp extra-virgin olive oil
- 2-6-ounce cans chunk light tuna, drained
- 2 tbsp lemon juice
- 1 15-ounce can cannellini white beans, rinsed
- ¼ tsp salt, to taste
- Freshly ground pepper, to taste

Directions

1. Take out a medium bowl and combine tomatoes, tuna, beans, lemon juice, scallions, oil, salt, and pepper.
2. Mix them well and serve.
3. Refrigerate if you are planning to serve later.

Nutrition: Calories: 199, Protein: 16.5 g, Total Fat: 8.8 g, Carbs: 19.8 g, Cholesterol: 7 mg 180.

Avocado Mango Mash

Preparation Time: 10 minutes
Cooking Time: 0 minutes
Servings: 4
Ingredients

- 2 minced garlic cloves
- 3 avocados, cubed
- ½ jalapeno, chopped without seeds
- 1 mango, cubed
- 1 tsp ground cumin
- ¼ cup sliced green onion
- ¼ tsp each sea salt &black pepper
- Cayenne pepper, to taste
- 1 lime's juice
- 2 tbsp fresh cilantro, chopped

Directions

1. Add all fixings to a bowl, and mash to your desired consistency.
2. Serve and enjoy.

Nutrition: Calories: 256, Protein: 18 g, Carbs: 4.5 g, Fat: 13.4 g, Cholesterol: 78 mg

Strawberry Cheesecake Cheeseball

Preparation Time: 10 minutes + chilling time
Cooking Time: 0 minutes
Servings: 8
Ingredients

- ¾ cup no-calorie sweetener
- ½ cup strawberry jelly, sugar-free
- ½ tbsp vanilla extract
- 16 oz Greek yogurt cream cheese, low-fat
- 2 cups high fiber cereal
- 3 packed protein powder
- 2 cups diced strawberries

Directions

1. Add cream cheese and beat with protein powder, vanilla, and sweetener in a bowl. Drain the jelly and add to the cream cheese mixture with strawberries.
2. Fold it in. Transfer to a plastic wrap and make it into a ball. Keep in the fridge for 3 hours. Serve with graham crackers.

Nutrition: Calories: 278, Protein: 13 g, Carbs: 5 g, Fat: 11.3 g, Cholesterol: 9 mg

Caprese Snack Bowl

Preparation Time: 10 minutes
Cooking Time: 0 minutes
Servings: 4
Ingredients

- 10 to 12 cherry tomatoes, halved
- 1 tsp balsamic glaze
- ¼ tsp each sea salt & black pepper
- 1 tsp fresh basil, sliced
- 2 sticks light mozzarella, cut into 1" pieces
- 1 tsp olive oil

Directions

1. In a bowl, mix basil, tomatoes, and cheese.
2. Add salt and pepper and oil, and toss to coat. Serve.

Nutrition: Calories: 78, Protein: 11g, Carbs: 2g, Fat: 4g, Cholesterol: 7 mg

Chicken Salad Cucumber Bites

Preparation Time: 15 minutes
Cooking Time: 0 minutes
Servings: 4
Ingredients
- ½ cucumber, sliced into circles
- ⅓ cup red onion, diced
- ⅓ cup light mayonnaise
- 1 chicken breast, cooked & diced
- Salt & pepper, to taste

Directions
1. In a bowl, add all fixings except for cucumber slices.
2. Mix and spoon onto cucumber slices, and serve.

Nutrition: Calories: 55, Protein: 21 g, Carbs: 3g, Fat: 2g, Cholesterol: 7 mg

Mock Mashed Potatoes

Preparation Time: 10 minutes

Cooking Time: 10 minutes

Servings: 4

Ingredients

- 8 oz frozen cauliflower
- 1 pack chicken bouillon soup, low-sodium

Directions

1. Cook the cauliflower as you like until tender. Mash and mix with half of the soup pack.
2. Mix and serve.

Nutrition: Calories: 87, Protein: 12 g, Carbs: 10 g, Fat: 1.1 g

Chapter 12 Desserts Recipes

Honey Walnut Bars

Preparation Time: 20 minutes

Cooking Time: 30 minutes

Servings: 8

Ingredients

- 5 oz puff pastry
- ½ cup water
- 3 tbsp liquid honey
- 1 tsp Erythritol
- ⅓ cup butter, softened
- ½ cup walnuts, chopped
- 1 tsp olive oil

Directions

1. Roll up the puff pastry and cut it into 6 sheets.
2. Then brush the tray with olive oil and arrange the first puff pastry sheet inside.
3. Grease it with butter gently and sprinkle with walnuts.
4. Repeat the same steps with 4 puff pastry sheets.
5. Then sprinkle the last layer with walnuts and Erythritol and cover with the 6th puff pastry sheet.
6. Cut the baklava on the servings.
7. Bake the baklava for 30 minutes.
8. Meanwhile, bring to boil liquid honey and water.
9. When the baklava is cooked, remove it from the oven.
10. Pour hot honey liquid over baklava and let it cool till room

temperature.

Nutrition: Calories: 243, Fat: 4.4 g, Fiber: 19.4 g, Carbs: 15.9 g, Protein: 1.9 g, Cholesterol: 12 mg

Yogurt Parfait

Preparation Time: 5 minutes

Cooking Time: 0 minutes

Servings: 1

Ingredients

- 1 oz blueberries
- 2 tbsp Plain yogurt
- ½ tsp vanilla extract

Directions

1. Mix up together Plain yogurt and vanilla extract.
2. Then put ½ oz of blueberries in the glass.
3. Cover the berries with ½ part of Plain yogurt.
4. Then add the layer of berries.
5. Top parfait with remaining Plain yogurt.

Nutrition: Calories: 44, Fat: 0.4 g, Fiber: 0.4 g, Carbs: 6.9 g, Protein: 1.9 g, Cholesterol: 12 mg

Raspberry Tart

Preparation Time: 15 minutes
Cooking Time: 10 minutes
Servings: 6
Ingredients

- 3 tbsp butter, softened
- 1 cup wheat flour, whole wheat
- 1 tsp baking powder
- 1 egg, beaten
- 4 tbsp pistachio paste
- 2 tbsp raspberry jam

Directions

1. Knead the dough: combine the softened butter, flour, baking powder, and egg. You should get the non-sticky and very soft dough.
2. Put the dough in the springform pan and flatten it with the help of your fingertips until you get the pie crust.
3. Bake it for 10 minutes at 365°F.
4. After this, spread the pie crust with raspberry jam and then with pistachio paste.
5. Bake the tart at 365°F for another 10 minutes.
6. Cool the cooked tart and cut on the servings.

Nutrition: Calories: 311, Fat: 11.4 g, Fiber: 1.4 g, Carbs: 14.9 g, Protein: 1.9 g, Cholesterol: 65 mg

Quinoa Energy Bars

Preparation Time: 20 minutes
Cooking Time: 15 minutes
Servings: 8
Ingredients
- ½ cup puffed quinoa
- ¼ cup oats
- 2 oz dark chocolate
- 2 tbsp almond butter
- ¾ cup maple syrup
- 1 tbsp butter
- 1 tbsp coconut flakes

Directions
1. Place dark chocolate, butter, maple syrup, and almond butter in the saucepan.
2. Melt the mixture and add oats, puffed quinoa, and coconut flakes.
3. Mix up well and remove it from the heat.
4. After this, line the baking tray with baking paper and transfer the quinoa mixture to it.
5. Flatten it well with the help of the spatula and cut on the bars (8 pieces).
6. Bake the quinoa bars for 10 minutes at 365°F.
7. After this, remove the tray with quinoa bars from the oven and cool well.

Nutrition: Calories: 240, Fat: 6.4 g, Fiber: 1.4 g, Carbs: 29.9 g, Protein: 1.9 g, Cholesterol: 12 mg

Cinnamon Stuffed Peaches

Preparation Time: 10 minutes
Cooking Time: 15 minutes
Servings: 4
Ingredients

- 4 peaches, pitted, halved
- 2 tbsp ricotta cheese
- 2 tbsp liquid honey
- ¾ cup water
- ½ tsp vanilla extract
- ¾ tsp ground cinnamon
- 1 tbsp almonds, sliced
- ¾ tsp saffron

Directions

1. Pour water into the saucepan and bring to a boil.
2. Add vanilla extract, saffron, ground cinnamon, and liquid honey.
3. Cook the liquid until the honey is melted.
4. Then remove it from the heat.
5. Put the halved peaches in the hot honey liquid.
6. Meanwhile, make the filling: mix up together ricotta cheese, vanilla extract, and sliced almonds.
7. Remove the peaches from the honey liquid and arrange them in the plate. Fill 4 peach halves with ricotta filling and cover them with remaining peach halves.
8. Sprinkle the cooked dessert with a liquid honey mixture gently.

Nutrition: Calories: 213, Fat: 1.4 g, Fiber: 2.4 g, Carbs: 23.9 g, Protein: 1.9 g, Cholesterol: 23 mg

Blueberry Muffins

Preparation Time: 15 minutes
Cooking Time: 25 minutes
Servings: 4
Ingredients

- 1 cup whole wheat flour
- 1 tsp baking powder
- ¼ cup blueberries
- 1 tsp vanilla extract
- 1 tbsp butter, softened
- ¾ cup sour cream
- 1 tbsp Erythritol
- Cooking spray

Directions

1. In the mixing bowl combine wheat flour and baking powder.
2. Then add sour cream, vanilla extract, butter, and Erythritol.
3. Stir the mixture well until smooth. You should get a thick batter. Add more sour cream if needed.
4. After this, add blueberries and carefully stir the batter.
5. Spray the muffin molds with the cooking spray.
6. Fill ½ part of every muffin mold with batter.
7. Preheat the oven to 365°F.
8. Place the muffins in the prepared oven and cook them for 25 minutes.
9. The cooked muffins will have a golden color surface.

Nutrition: Calories: 241, Fat: 12.4 g, Fiber: 1.4 g, Carbs: 24.9 g, Protein: 1.9 g, Cholesterol: 78 mg

Lime Grapes and Apples

Preparation Time: 10 minutes

Cooking Time: 25 minutes

Servings: 2

Ingredients
- ½ cup red grapes
- 2 apples
- 1 tsp lime juice
- 1 tsp Erythritol
- 3 tbsp water

Directions
1. Line the baking tray with baking paper.
2. Then cut the apples in halves and remove the seeds with the help of the scooper.
3. Cut the apple halves into 2 parts more.
4. Arrange all fruits in the tray in 1 layer, drizzle with water, and bake for 20 minutes at 375°F.
5. Flip the fruits to another side after 10 minutes of cooking.
6. Then remove them from the oven and sprinkle them with lime juice and Erythritol.
7. Return the fruits to the oven and bake for 5 minutes more.
8. Serve the cooked dessert hot or warm.

Nutrition: Calories: 142, Fat: 4.4 g, Fiber: 5.4 g, Carbs: 40.9 g, Protein: 1.9 g, Cholesterol: 11 mg

Almond Citrus Muffins

Preparation Time: 10 minutes
Cooking Time: 40 minutes
Servings: 6
Ingredients

- 2 eggs, beaten
- 1 ½ cups whole wheat flour
- ½ cup almond meal
- 1 tsp vanilla extract
- 1 tbsp butter, softened
- 1 tsp orange zest, grated
- 1 tbsp orange juice
- ¾ cup Erythritol
- 1 oz orange pulp
- 1 tsp baking powder
- ½ tsp lime zest, grated
- Cooking spray

Directions

1. Make the muffin batter: combine together almond meal, eggs, whole wheat flour, vanilla extract, butter, orange zest, orange juice, and orange pulp.
2. Add lime zest and baking powder.
3. Then add Erythritol.
4. With the help of the hand mixer mix up the ingredients.
5. When the mixture is soft and smooth, it is done.
6. Spray the muffin molds with cooking spray from inside and preheat the

7   oven to 365°F.
8   Fill ½ part of every muffin mold with muffin batter and transfer them to the oven.
9   Cook the muffins for 30 minutes.
10 Then check if the muffins are cooked by piercing them with a toothpick (if it is dry, the muffins are cooked; if it is not dry, bake the muffins for 5 to 7 minutes more.)

Nutrition: Calories: 204, Fat: 7.4 g, Fiber: 1.4 g, Carbs: 57.9 g, Protein: 1.9 g, Cholesterol: 12 mg

Butter Cookies

Preparation Time: 15 minutes
Cooking Time: 15 minutes
Servings: 6
Ingredients

- ⅓ cup wheat flour
- ¼ cup coconut flour
- 2 egg whites
- 3 tbsp butter, softened
- ½ tsp vanilla extract
- 1 tbsp Erythritol

Directions

1. In the mixing bowl combine Erythritol, wheat flour, and coconut flour.
2. Whisk the egg whites in the separated bowl till you get soft peaks.
3. After this, combine the wheat mixture and egg whites.
4. Add vanilla extract and softened butter.
5. Carefully mix up the cookie mixture with the help of a fork/spoon.
6. After this, line the baking tray with baking paper.
7. Make 6 balls from the coconut mixture, press them a little with the help of the palm and arrange them in the tray. Make enough space for every cookie in the tray.
8. Bake the cookies for 15 minutes at 375°F.
9. When the cookies are lightly golden but not brown, they are cooked.
10. Chill them well and store them in the glass jar.

Nutrition: Calories: 103, Fat: 6.4 g, Fiber: 1.4 g, Carbs: 11.9 g, Protein: 1.9 g, Cholesterol: 11 mg

Minty Tart

Preparation Time: 20 minutes
Cooking Time: 30 minutes
Servings: 6
Ingredients

- 1 cup tart cherries, pitted
- 1 cup wheat flour, whole grain
- ⅓ cup butter, softened
- ½ tsp baking powder
- 1 tbsp Erythritol
- ¼ tsp dried mint
- ¾ tsp salt

Directions

1. Mix up together wheat flour and butter.
2. Add baking powder and salt. Knead the soft dough.
3. Then place the dough in the freezer for 10 minutes.
4. When the dough is solid, remove it from the freezer and grate with the help of the grater. Place ¼ part of the grated dough in the freezer.
5. Sprinkle the spring form pan with the remaining dough and place tart cherries on it.
6. Sprinkle the cherries with Erythritol and dried mint and cover with ¼ part of the dough from the freezer.
7. Bake the cake for 30 minutes at 365°F. The cooked tart will have a golden brown surface.

Nutrition: Calories: 177, Fat: 4.4 g, Fiber: 7.4 g, Carbs: 21.9 g, Protein: 1.9 g, Cholesterol: 12 mg

Lemon Chocolate Cookies

Preparation Time: 15 minutes
Cooking Time: 18 minutes
Servings: 10
Ingredients

- 4 tbsp olive oil
- ½ tsp almond extract
- 1 egg, beaten
- ⅓ cup Erythritol
- ½ tsp baking soda
- ½ tsp lemon juice
- 3 oz dark chocolate, chopped
- 1 cup flour, whole grain

Directions

1. Put olive oil, almond extract, egg, and Erythritol in the food processor.
2. Blend the mixture until smooth and add baking soda, lemon juice, and flour.
3. Blend the mixture. You should get soft but non-sticky dough. Add more flour if needed.
4. Then add chopped dark chocolate and mix up the dough with the help of the fingertips.
5. Line the baking tray with baking paper.
6. Scoop the dough into the balls with the help of the scooper and place them in the tray.
7. Bake the cookies at 365°F for 18 minutes.

Nutrition: Calories: 146, Fat: 4.4 g, Fiber: 8.4 g, Carbs: 22.9 g, Protein: 1.9 g, Cholesterol: 11 mg

Chocolate Brownies With Almond Butter

Preparation Time: 10 minutes
Cooking Time: 25 minutes
Servings: 16 brownies

Ingredients

- Nonstick cooking spray
- ½ cup cocoa powder
- 1 tbsp ground flaxseed
- ½ tsp ground instant coffee
- ¼ tsp baking soda
- ½ cup agave nectar
- ½ cup almond butter
- 2 large eggs
- ¼ cup melted coconut oil
- 1 tsp vanilla extract

Directions

1. Warm the oven to 325°F. Coat an 8x8-inch glass baking dish with cooking spray.
2. Place the cocoa powder, flaxseed, instant coffee, baking soda, almond butter, coconut oil, eggs, vanilla extract, and agave nectar in a high-speed blender or food processor.
3. Blend on medium-high until smooth. Pour the batter into the baking dish. Bake within 25 minutes or until a toothpick in the middle comes out clean.
4. Let cool for 10 minutes before cutting into 16 squares.

Nutrition: Calories: 124, Protein: 3 g, Carbs: 11g, Fat: 9g, Cholesterol: 11 mg

Lemon Blackberry Frozen Yogurt

Preparation Time: 10 minutes + chilling time
Cooking Time: 0 minutes
Servings: 4 cups

Ingredients

- 4 cups frozen blackberries
- ½ cup low-fat Greek yogurt
- 1 lemon juice
- 2 tsp liquid stevia
- Fresh mint leaves, for garnish

Directions

1. Add the blackberries, yogurt, lemon juice, and stevia to your blender or a food processor. Blend until smooth for about 5 minutes.
2. Serve immediately or freeze in your airtight container and use within 3 weeks. Garnish with fresh mint leaves.

Nutrition: Calories: 68, Protein: 3g, Carbs: 15g, Fat: 0g, Cholesterol: 12 mg

Skinny Mug Brownie

Preparation Time: 10 minutes

Cooking Time: 1 minute

Servings: 3

Ingredients

- 1 tbsp cocoa powder, unsweetened
- 2 packets sweeteners
- 2 tbsp all-purpose flour
- 3 tbsp almond milk

Directions

1. Place all ingredients in a microwave-safe mug. Mix with a fork or small whisk.
2. Microwave on high for 60 seconds. Enjoy.

Nutrition: Calories: 97, Protein: 1.2 g, Carbs: 9.2 g, Fat: 2.2 g, Cholesterol: 11 mg

Carrot Cake

Preparation Time: 15 minutes

Cooking Time: 15 minutes

Servings: 2

Ingredients

- ¼ cup flour
- ½ tsp cinnamon
- ¼ tsp baking powder
- ⅛ tsp baking soda
- ⅓ cup canned carrots, drained
- ⅛ tsp salt
- 1 ½ tbsp brown sugar
- Pinch of uncut stevia/1 tbsp sugar
- 1 tbsp milk
- ½ tsp ginger or 2 tsp flax meal (optional)
- 1 tbsp oil
- ¼ tsp pure vanilla extract

Directions

1. In your small bowl, mix the dry ingredients except for the carrots. In your blender, mix all the wet ingredients, including the carrots.
2. Mix the dry mixture with the wet mixture, and stir. Pour this mixture into a greased little dish.
3. Cook in the oven at 350°F for around 15 minutes. Let it cool before trying to pop out.

Nutrition: Calories: 70, Protein: 2.5 g, Carbs: 17 g, Fat: 0.5 g, Cholesterol: 11 mg

Mini Plum Cakes

Preparation Time: 15 minutes
Cooking Time: 20 to 25 minutes
Servings: 12
Ingredients

- ¾ cup all-purpose flour
- ¼ flaxseed meal
- 1 ½ tsp baking powder
- ¼ tsp kosher salt
- 3 tbsp unsalted butter, at room temperature
- 2 tbsp avocado
- ⅓ cup sugar
- 1 large egg
- ⅔ cup low-fat milk
- 1 tsp finely grated lemon zest
- 1 tsp vanilla extract
- 1 plum (or any stone fruit), pitted and cut into thin slices
- 2 tbsp raw sugar (optional)

Directions

1. Warm the oven to 350°F. Use nonstick spray to coat the muffin pan. Whisk baking powder, flaxseed meal, flour, and salt in a bowl. Put aside.

2. Use an electric processor to beat avocado, butter, and sugar in another bowl until light and fluffy, within 2 minutes. Add egg, lemon zest, plus vanilla, and beat until combined.

3. With your mixer on low speed, add dry fixings in 3 additions alternating with milk in 2 additions, beginning and ending

with dry ingredients.

4. Pour batter evenly among muffin cups. Sprinkle plum slices and raw sugar on top. Bake for 20 to 25 minutes until golden.

5. Transfer the pan to your wire rack; let the pan cool for 5 minutes. Transfer the cakes to your rack and let them cool completely.

Nutrition: Calories: 113, Protein: 3g, Carbs: 14g, Fat: 5g, Cholesterol: 23 mg

Conclusion

Surgery for gastric bypass can frequently save lives. Expect to lose weight more quickly than in the past, experience fewer co-morbidities (some even before the surgery!), and feel and look better than in the past. However, in order to be successful (over time), you will probably need to change some behaviors, including your eating habits.

These adjustments don't have to be done by you alone! Locate a surgical facility that can help you get the support you require to make these changes permanent. Find a support network, either offline or online.

There are many benefits to connecting with people who are experiencing the same thing as you. If you need assistance after surgery with any aspect of your life, you can also get it from peers and professionals.

The gastric bypass diet can help you get better after surgery and gradually transition to a healthy eating routine that will enable you to lose weight. After having weight loss surgery, keep in mind that you might not lose all of the weight you lost or you might gain it back if you resume your old eating habits. Making healthy food choices after surgery begins with understanding what you can and cannot eat. Two factors make the initial several weeks after gastric bypass surgery crucial:

A pre-op liquid diet is advised by the majority of surgery clinics to reduce the amount of fat around the liver and spleen. Before having gastric bypass surgery, a preoperative liquid diet must normally be followed for 2 weeks.

Your treatment will be performed near your stomach, which is where your liver is situated.

www.ingramcontent.com/pod-product-compliance
Lightning Source LLC
Chambersburg PA
CBHW050358120526
44590CB00015B/1732